SUPERMAN ®

THE
SOURCEBOOK

TABLE OF CONTENTS

THE SUPERMAN SOURCEBOOK

© 1987 DC Comics Inc.
All Rights Reserved.
Published by Mayfair Games Inc.

Author: Steve Crow, Chris Mortika
Editor: Jacqueline Leeper

Cover Art: *Pencils and Inks:* John Byrne, *Color:* Bob LeRose
Interior Art: DC Staff
Maps: DC Staff, Jerry O'Malley, Greg Scott
Editorial Assistance: Jonatha Ariadne Caspian, Troy Denning

 is a registered trademark of DC Comics Inc., used under license by Mayfair Games Inc.

 is a trademark of DC Comics Inc., used under license by Mayfair Games Inc.

 is a registered trademark of Mayfair Games Inc.

Mayfair Games Inc. • P.O. Box 48539 • Niles, IL • 60648

This book is respectfully dedicated to E. Nelson Bridwell, chronicler and creator of much of the Superman mythos.

We gratefully acknowledge the assistance of: Robert Feldacker, David Martin, Richard Morrissey, Kathy Tomash, Alan Turniansky, and Susan Wise.

happy
birthday
superman

5

HOW TO USE THIS BOOK

After the Crisis on Infinite Earths, DC revised Superman's Character. He is no longer the omnipotent, untouchable demi-god of legend. Instead, he is a very human man who happens to possess extraordinary powers. The considerable differences between the abilities of the two versions has a profound impact upon the *DC Heroes Role-Playing Game*. The purpose of this book is to illustrate those differences for gamemasters and players in as much detail as possible.

As a sourcebook on Superman, this book contains both background material and game-related information about Superman, his friends, and his foes. Gamemasters who prefer writing their own adventures will find this sourcebook helpful since, in addition to Characters' backgrounds and statistics, it includes information about essential aspects of Superman's existence. For example, there are sections detailing the Phantom Zone and Krypton.

There are certain Characters, other than Superman, whose statistics are somewhat different from those given in the Gamemaster's Manual and/or in previous modules. This is intentional, as the DC Universe is ongoing and new developments always occur. For example, a specific Character may have learned Martial Arts since the Character's statistics were last included in a module. Thus, the Martial Artist Skill can be included in the Character's most recent statistics.

Some Power descriptions in this book, such as Time Travel, are also different from other descriptions of the same Powers. This is also intentional. The differences reflect an updated perception of how these powers operate in the DC universe.

The *Introduction* and *Table of Contents* describes how this book is broken down into sections.

How to Read the New Gadget Box

The gadgetry rules have undergone some changes. Any Character's equipment listed in this book will use the new format for gadgets. Given in this section is a brief explanation of this format. For details on the new gadgetry rules and a list of new gadgets, refer to the *Hardware Handbook*.

The gadget box looks similar to the Character statistic box used in all the modules, but there are some important differences.

Gadget Box		
DEX:	STR:	BODY:
INT:	WILL:	MIND:
INFL:	AURA:	SPIRIT:
INITIATIVE:	HERO POINTS:	
CHARGES:		
COST:	HPs + $	

OMNI—GADGET
CLASS A:
CLASS B:
CLASS C:
CLASS D:
CHARGES:
COST:*HPs + $

Attributes are listed by class: Physical, Mental, Mystical. If a gadget has a value for one attribute in a class, it must have values for all of them, even if the value is 0. If a gadget does not have any attributes in a particular class, that line will be missing from the box. A gadget with no attributes in a class cannot be attacked with a Power that affects that class.

For example, a villain cannot use Control on Nightwing's combat disk, because the combat disk has only Physical attributes, and no Mental attributes.

A gadget must have APs in each Mental attribute to have Artificial Intelligence. In order for a gadget to have free will, that gadget must have APs in *each* Physical, Mental, and Mystical attribute.

Initiative is only listed for those gadgets that have free will. A gadget that does not have all three classes of attributes (and at least 1 AP in each of the Mystical attributes) cannot decide for itself what action to take and then execute the plan: therefore, it does not have an Initiative.

Hero Points are only given to gadgets that have free will.

Charges are listed in the box to remind you that this is a gadget (even if it is also a Character), and must have routine maintenance and refueling.

The number of charges represents the amount of energy in a gadget's reservoir. **One charge is burned each time a dice roll is required when the gadget is using its attributes or standard Powers or Skills. If a gadget uses Automatic Powers, it burns one charge for each AP of time its Powers are used.** A gadget may use more than one attribute, Power, or Skill during one AP.

Some gadgets have an external or internal power source; this is indicated as EPS (*external power source*) or IPS (*internal power source*). NA means *not applicable*. In all of these cases, players are not required to keep track of charges burned.

Cost is the price in Hero Points and cash that a hero must pay for a prototype device of this nature. Notice that the gadgets in this book are in prototype form. For an individual Character to build a prototype gadget, s/he must also build or acquire the manufacturing equipment and testing facilities; there is also a certain amount of time required to develop a gadget. In most cases, it is much less trouble to buy the gadget from a retailer, an inventor, a government . . . or from whomever has access to it.

Cash Costs are given with the following abbreviations:

K = thousand. ($38K means $38,000.)

M = million. ($2.574M means $2,574,000.)

B = billion. ($1.039B means $1,039,000,000.)

T = trillion. ($8.005T means $8,005,000,000,000.)

Q = quadrillion. ($6.5Q means $6,500,000,000,000,000.)

QN = quintillion. ($4.9QN means $4,900,000,000,000,000,000.)

Omni-Gadgets, which are gadgets whose exact Powers and attributes are unknown, have their own boxes. If a class of attributes is not listed for an omni-gadget, the gadget does not have that category of attributes, and cannot be attacked with Powers that affect them.

When an omni-gadget is not functioning, its BODY is the number of APs assigned to class A (Physical attributes).

An omni-gadget's class indicates the type of device that the omni-gadget can turn into.

OMNI-GADGET CLASSES

Class A . . . **Physical attributes (DEX, STR, BODY)**
Class B . . . . **Mental attributes (INT, WILL, MIND)**
Class C . . . . **Powers**
Class D . . **The ability to substitute its own APs for its user's attributes**

All omni-gadgets must possess class A. The inventor may assign 0 APs to class A if s/he wishes. Omni-gadgets never possess Skills or Mystical attributes. In addition, if a gadgeteer anticipates the need for Powers with a Mental link, s/he requires an omni-gadget with class B. *Omni-gadgets never possess powers with Mystical links.*

Converting New Gadgets to the Old Rules

If you do not have the *Hardware Handbook* or prefer to use the old gadgetry rules, use the process outlined below to convert the new gadgets in this book to the old rules.

Leave all attribute, Power, and/or Skill scores as they appear in the new statistics. You need only to convert Charges to Uses and Durations; use the following procedure:

1. Count the number of attributes, Powers, and Skills the gadget must use constantly to fulfill its purpose.
2. Divide the total number of Charges by this number. The result is the gadget's Duration.
3. Count the number of attributes, Powers, and Skills the gadget does not use constantly to fulfill its purpose. This is the number of the gadget's Uses.

Adjust these numbers as you feel is appropriate.

Because of the differences in the underlying philosophies of the old gadgetry rules and the new, especially in the areas of attribute use and energy supply, it is impossible to develop an exact conversion method. These procedures will yield close approximations of the same gadget in the two systems.

COLUMN SHIFTS

• A *negative (-)* column shift to the OV and/or RV is to the *left* on the Action Table and makes an action easier.

• A *positive (+)* column to the OV and/or RV is to the *right* on the Action Table and makes an action more difficult.

ABBREVIATIONS

AP	Attribute Point
AURA	Aura Attribute
AV	Acting Value
BODY	Body Attribute
DEX	Dexterity Attribute
EV	Effect Value
GM	Gamemaster
HP(s)	Hero Point(s)
INFL	Influence Attribute
INT	Intelligence Attribute
MIND	Mind Attribute
NA	Not Applicable
NPC(s)	Non-Player Character(s)
OV	Opposing Value
RAP(s)	Result Attribute Point(s)
RV	Resistance Value
SPIRIT	Spirit Attribute
STR	Strength Attribute
WILL	Willpower Attribute

THIS IS A JOB FOR...

SUP

He is one of the most famous fictional characters of all time. He has been immortalized in 1,800 issues of his own titles, in guest-starring roles in every DC Comic from Black Lightning to Wonder Woman, in a 1950's television program, three major movies, a number of 1940's serials, at least four cartoon programs and short films, a radio program, a newspaper strip, three novels, a Broadway musical, and innumerable advertising campaigns.

Probably nine people in ten know who Superman is. Most of us who know of the Man of Steel know that he came from the planet Krypton and that he fights for Truth, Justice and the American Way. The stylized *S* symbol in red-on-yellow is internationally recognized; the Superman legend has been translated into nearly every language in the world.

A man with incredible strength, indestructibility, and the ability to fly is a powerful fantasy. The universal appeal of this fantasy has been the basis for Superman's popularity throughout his 50-year career.

Superman is also legendary because, in his Clark Kent personna, he represents the typical "everyman." Clark Kent is not heroic; he is sometimes ill-fated in love, not very lucky, and usually shy of danger. But, when Clark Kent becomes Superman, he demonstrates that he can rise above his failings, becoming a heroic, virile figure who

is loved and adored by the public.

Superman embodies the fight to uphold all that is true and good. He is known world-wide as a champion of justice and fair play who fights crime whenever and wherever he finds it. Yet, unlike many other heroes, he does not spend all of his efforts fighting evil. Superman is as famous for performing good deeds — such as fighting fires or rescuing stranded pets — as he is for jailing criminals.

In his comic book universe, Superman is surrounded by one of the largest and richest supporting casts of any fictional character. The names of Lois Lane, Jimmy Olsen, and Perry White are as well known as Superman himself.

The Man of Steel has starred in several DC Comics titles throughout the years. These include: *Action Comics*, *Superman*, *DC Comics Presents*, and *Adventure*. He has appeared with many other DC characters such as the Batman, the Flash, and Wonder Woman and has been a member of the Justice League of America.

DC Comic's treatment of Superman has covered his career as a baby, a boy, an adult, and an old man. We have seen future stories and "dream" stories in which Superman has died, married Lois Lane, lost his powers permanently and become a normal man, or disappeared

into the mists of time. Not content with one Man of Steel, DC has created a Superman of Earth-2 (one of the parallel worlds of the DC Comics universe) who has aged and married.

Over the years Superman has accumulated an extensive history. DC recently decided that Superman needed "revitalization" and redid the character. The Superman that emerged from this remake is certainly a changed character. No longer an isolated figure of epic proportion, Superman now grapples with the problems of common men as well as matters more suited to his tremendous abilities. Is he paying enough attention to his girlfriend? Do his aging parents understand the pressures which prevent him from spending more time with them? In addition to the emphasis on his human concerns, the new Superman is not as powerful as he once was. On several occasions, he has actually been stunned, and there are now definite limits to his strength.

This book, which honors Superman's 50th anniversary, describes the old Superman and his world. During the next 50 years, the new Man of Steel is sure to be as successful as the old. That means his world will rapidly become as rich and action-packed as the old Superman's world. We want to ensure that the wonder of the old Superman is preserved.

ABOUT THIS BOOK . . .

At one time, there were a number of parallel worlds in the DC Comics universe. Earth-1, on which most "modern" DC Characters live or have lived, and Earth-2, on which most of the DC Characters from the 40's lived before it was obliterated, are two of these worlds. In 1985, DC Comics created the *Crisis on Infinite Earths* to simplify matters by wiping out most of these parallel Earths. Earth-1 and Earth-2 merged as a result of the Crisis, and the new Superman appeared.

Based on the DC universe before the *Crisis on Infinite Earths*, this book is divided into two basic sections: **Pre-Crisis** and **Earth-2**. It does not discuss the Post-Crisis Superman at all.

The **Pre-Crisis** section applies to the way things were on Earth-1 before the *Crisis on Infinite Earths* occurred; it describes the more powerful version of Superman that existed before the cataclysmic realignment of the DC universe. It outlines the history of Krypton, its survivors, and many of Superman's friends and foes from that time. Also included in this first section are details about Superman's equipment, a glossary of Kryptonese words, maps of Krypton, maps of the Fortress of Solitude, and a chapter describing the Phantom Zone.

The second (**Earth-2**) section does the same thing for the world of the Earth-2 Superman. However, it only covers the Earth-2 Superman's history and his friends and foes.

With this sourcebook, a Gamemaster has the necessary background materials for campaigns with either the Earth-2 Superman of the 1940's or the more powerful Pre-Crisis Man of Steel.

FOR MORE INFORMATION . . .

There have been several DC Comics titles which deal with the Earth-2 Superman and the Post-Crisis Superman. The following are the major ones:

Who's Who
Action Comics
DC Comics Presents
Adventure
Jimmy Olsen
Superman Family

There are also several Superman team-up issues (i.e. *Superman/Batman*, *Superman/the Flash*, etc.).

NEW POWERS

The following Powers were included in past modules but were not included in the Gamemaster's Manual. There are Characters and gadgets in this book that have these Powers. Therefore, they have been included here for ease of reference.

ADAPTATION *Mental*

LINK:	INT
RANGE:	Special
TYPE:	Special
BASE COST:	85

Adaptation allows a Character to duplicate any other Power or Skill available in the campaign. However, a Power may only be duplicated if the Character attempting an Adaptation has seen the target Character use that Power before. The Character may use any combination of Powers as long as the total APs do not exceed the APs of Adaptation.

The Character using the Adaptation Power must concentrate for one phase before the duplicated Power can take effect.

A Power Limitation must be taken when purchasing this Power. No extra Hero Points are received for this Limitation.

CLAWS *Physical*

LINK:	DEX
RANGE:	Touch
TYPE:	Standard
BASE COST:	15

The Claws Power is for Characters who have claws or other natural sharpened-attack forms (e.g. teeth, tusks, etc.). The APs of Claws are treated as the AV/EV of the attacking Character. Claws APs can also be treated as STR for cutting (but not lifting or moving) materials.

CONTINUUM CONTROL *Mental*

LINK:	WILL
RANGE:	Normal
TYPE:	Automatic
BASE COST:	175

Continuum Control allows a Character to tinker with the nature of matter and have some control over the space/time continuum.

As it is an Automatic Power, the APs of the Power are the RAPs. The RAPs of Continuum Control are the APs of the Power that is mimicked. Continuum Control may be used as one or more of these Powers: Bio-Energy Blast, Damage Transference, Matter Manipulation, Regathering, Regeneration, Time Travel, Teleportation, or Transformation.

It is important to note that use of Continuum Control takes a phase. A Character must use Continuum Control for a phase, and then mimic a Power in the next phase with the RAPs of Continuum Control.

The RAPs of Continuum Control can be distributed amongst the mimicked Powers as the Player wishes as long as the total APs of all Powers mimicked in a phase does not exceed the RAPs of Continuum Control. For example, a Character with 10 APs of Continuum Control could have a Bio-Energy Blast of 6 APs and a Teleportation of 4 APs in the same phase.

The Powers mimicked by Continuum Control function in the following way:

Bio-Energy Blast: As described in Powers and Skills.

Note that if a Character combines Teleportation and Bio-Energy Blast on the same target, he will be entering Killing Combat. In this case the target is attacked by the Bio-Energy Blast and (if there are RAPs) the target's molecules are blasted over a distance equal to the range of the Teleportation (assuming the Teleportation was successful). If a Character has his current BODY reduced to below 0 in this way, then he is certain to die. If the target Character has the Invulnerability Power, it is useless as the target's atoms are scattered in space. Recovery Rolls are not allowed, so the Character loses BODY until he is dead. The Regathering Power (see below) may be used to regather the scattered atoms of a Character who has been Bio-Energy Blasted and Teleported into oblivion.

Damage Transference: As described in Powers and Skills.

Matter Manipulation: As described in Powers and Skills.

Regathering: This allows a Character who has been scattered as described in Bio-Energy Blast above to be 'regrouped.' The Opposing Value is the Range APs of the Teleportation, which scattered his atoms when his current BODY was reduced below 0 by the Bio-Energy Blast. The Resistance Value is the BODY of the Character being regathered. If there are any Positive RAPs, the action is successful.

Regeneration: As described in Powers and Skills.

Teleportation: As described in Powers and Skills with the following exceptions: The Range of the Teleportation is Normal rather than +7 and the Character may Teleport any Character within Range, not just those within ten feet of him.

Time Travel: There are two distinct aspects of the use of Time Travel: going forward into the future and going back into the past.

If the target is sent into the future he may take all the actions his Character would normally take. The Opposing Value is the INT of the target and the Resistance Value is the BODY. The RAPs are the APs of time which the target Character is sent ahead into time.

When going backward in time, the target's body is considered to be thrown into limbo and his mind is left to observe. The target becomes a phantom that can only observe events and not affect or alter them. The Opposing Value is the INT of the target, and the Resistance Value is the MIND. The RAPs are the APs of time that the target Character is sent back in time.

In either case, the target has to be brought back by the attacking Character or he has to fight the actual Acting and Effect Values of Time Travel (the APs of the Power plus the Hero Points used) with his INT and WILL. The actual Acting and Effect Values are used as the Opposing and Resistance Values in this case.

If a Character wants to send himself into the past or future, the Opposing Value is 0 and the Resistance Value is the BODY if the Character is going into the future or the MIND if the Character is going into the past.

Transformation: Works in the same manner as Matter Manipulation, except that it also works on living creatures and organic materials.

DISINTEGRATION *Physical*

LINK:	AURA
RANGE:	Normal
TYPE:	Standard
BASE COST:	40

Disintegration breaks the molecular bonding of an object, causing the structure to dissolve into component elements.

Treat the use of this Power as a Physical attack; the target's BODY is the OV/RV. Disintegration works similarly to Poison Touch. Once a successful attack has been made, the target is attacked during each subsequent phase by the APs of Disintegration. The attacks continue until the target's BODY is reduced to its negative value (and is totally Disintegrated) or an action check fails.

If the target has still not been Disintegrated, the attacker may make another Disintegration attempt when the target has stopped taking damage from the previous attack. A partially Disintegrated target will take twice as many phases to solidify as it did to dissolve, unless a "healing" repair attempt is made. The object may not move, be moved, or be used until it is solid again (the molecular structure is still unstable). If the object is moved it will automatically Disintegrate again and another repair attempt

11

must be made.

If used against another Character, the user enters Killing Combat. A Character attacked with Disintegration who is not instantaneously killed can be healed with Regeneration while s/he is losing BODY APs.

DUMB LUCK *Mystical*

LINK:	INFL
RANGE:	Self
TYPE:	Standard
BASE COST:	60

Use of Dumb Luck is a Simple Action. A Character using Dumb Luck rolls against his or her own Mystical Attributes. The RAPs are the number of column shifts that that Character gets in his or her favor on his or her Resistance Value during that phase or Acting Value the next phase.

A Dumb Luck roll may be used to boost a subsequent Dumb Luck roll in the next phase and so on as long as the Player feels that the dice are on his or her side. If a Dumb Luck roll fails, all column shifts that have been accumulated are then used against that Character; in the next phase of battle (whenever that may be) all those column shifts may be used against the Character in whatever fashion the Gamemaster sees fit. Something, no matter how ludicrous, may happen, including safes falling out of the sky (even in the middle of a field), earthquakes, a giant koala bear walking through the city, etc.

NEUTRALIZE *Mental*

LINK:	WILL
RANGE:	Normal
TYPE:	Standard
BASE COST:	20

This Power allows a Character to negate one or more of an opponent's Powers. The OV and RV are the APs of the opposed Power. The RAPs are the length of time that the target loses the use of his or her Power. A victim may attempt to gain the use of his or her Power back sooner by making a Recovery Check, but the OV and RV are the RAPs of Neutralize, as the victim has taken no real damage.

This Power can also negate the Power-like functions of equipment or a Character's STR Attribute. A Multi-Attack may be made to affect more than one Power. The attack is treated as a Physical Attack against Physical Powers (and STR), a Mental Attack against Mental Powers, and a Mystical Attack against Mystical Powers.

PROJECTILE WEAPONS *Physical*

LINK:	STR
RANGE:	Normal
TYPE:	Standard
BASE COST:	15

Projectile Weapons allows a gadget or Character to fire projectiles. This Power is most commonly used for gadgets. For example, a submachine gun has 6 APs of Projectile Weapons, enabling it to fire bullets. An example of a Character with the Projectile Weapons Power is Porcupine Pete of the Legion of Substitute Heroes; he would use this Power to throw his quills. In either case, the APs of the Power act as the EV*.

Most Projectile Weapons have a Range, as stated in the *Player's Manual*. Unless otherwise determined, find the Range of a weapon or the Power by subtracting 3 from the APs of the Power for Short Range, and adding 1 to the APs of the Power for Long Range. Medium Range is in between the two figures.

Weapons are always used at full Power and may not be reduced in STR. Because of this restriction, a Character or gadget using the Projectile Weapons Power may be entering Killing Combat.

* Character may substitute his or her DEX for AV. Projectile Weapons *is not* used for the AV of an action check: any weapon without a DEX has an AV of 0.

REALITY CHECK *Mental*

LINK:	INT
RANGE:	Self
TYPE:	Standard
BASE COST:	30

Reality Check is a Power which may be used to determine if the story the Character is in is a hoax, a dream, an imaginary tale, or on which parallel Earth it is taking place. If your adventures or campaigns are nice solid down-to-reality types, read no further. However, if they include Ambush Bug, you've opened this book to the right place!

When a Reality Check is done, the GM's age acts as the OV/RV; the RAPs are how much information (in Knowledge Points) the GM tells the Player concerning what is really happening. The GM may use money to boost the OV and RV in the same manner that Hero Points are used. He does not have to give any money away, but he must show that it exists. One dollar (or nearest value in foreign countries) equals one Hero Point.

When a Reality Check backfires, there's usually trouble. The APs of Reality Check are the AV and EV in an attack on the Player Character's INT and MIND. This damage is *not* Killing Combat, and MIND will never go below zero in any case.

For more information on Reality Check, the intrepid GM should purchase the Ambush Bug adventure ***Don't Ask!*** by *Scott Jenkins*. It will provide you with more information on these Powers and give you an idea of the types of adventures in which they can be used.

REFLECTION/ DEFLECTION *Mental*

LINK:	WILL
RANGE:	Self
TYPE:	Special
BASE COST:	15

Reflection may be used to Deflect an attack made on the user. To "set" a Reflection, the user must use a Movement Action, thus immobilizing him- or herself for the rest of the phase. S/he may then use a Standard Action on up to two incoming attacks to Deflect and/or Reflect the attacks.

The OV and RV on a Reflection attempt are the APs of the incoming Power. With positive RAPs the attack is successfully Deflected. If the user wishes to redirect the beam at a new target of his choosing, an attack is made against the target (Reflection); the previously acquired RAPs then act as the new AV and EV. The OV/RV of the target are as appropriate.

Hero Points may be spent normally by both sides to affect the outcome, and Multi-Attacks can be made with normal penalties. A target for a Reflected attack does not have to be declared until the Reflecting Character needs to make an attack.

Powers with a range of Touch can be Reflected without the Reflecting Character touching the target. The Range of any other Reflected Power is the same as that Power's normal Range.

TIME TRAVEL *Mental*

LINK: NONE
RANGE: Special
TYPE: Standard
BASE COST: 1000

Time Travel allows the user to travel backwards or forwards through time. To understand the ramifications of this Power, we must digress a little into the theory of time.

Time can be pictured as a broad, constantly shifting stream; its various rivulets and channels make an interlocking web of possible realities. The pathways which a drop of water, or a time traveller, may take are multitudinous. Each path looks identical to the next, stretching forward and backward and interconnecting to any other path or point in the stream. A traveller could easily lose track of the path from which s/he departed.

Every day innumerable actions and decisions occur that set off new ripples in the timestream, as new possibilities add alternate realities. Most of these ripples have no lasting effect. They eventually recombine with the mainstream and leave no mark in history. But occasionally, events occur with consequences so severe or wide in scope that they become permanent features in the timestream, creating completely different realities. In time research, these phenomena are called Nexus Events, and the individuals whose combined presence and actions created these events are known as Nexus Personalities. An example of a Nexus Event is the development of the atom bomb in 1945, and an example of a Nexus Personality is Elizabeth I of England, who sponsored colonization in the new world and kept Spain from invading England.

But not all Nexus Events or Personalities make headlines and history books. Sometimes it is the failure of an event, or deeds of the children or students of a particular person, that are important to the timestream; their success or failure in an alternate reality may transform society in unexpected and disturbing ways.

With all of this in mind, these are the abilities and drawbacks of the Power of Time Travel:

If the user travels backward or forward to a time in which s/he is alive, s/he violates the Law of Duplication, and creates an infinite loop. The traveller repeats the events of his or her first visit endlessly, or until rescued by another time traveller.

For example, if Supergirl decided to time travel after she graduated from high school, and went back to her time at the Midvale Orphanage, she would have to relive the occurrences in her life between her reappearance at the orphanage and her high school graduation forever, or until another time traveller "broke" the cycle by intervening in the events.

However, if the time traveller goes to a period during which s/he is not alive, use the APs of Time Travel as AV/EV. Use the APs of time over which the Character wishes to travel as the OV/RV. If the RAPs are less than the APs of time travelled, the traveller's visit has had no lasting effect. If the RAPs are equal or greater than the APs of time travelled, then the time traveller has caused changes in the timestream. The RAPs are the amount of time that will have to pass before the timestream repairs those changes. Equal RAPs represent small changes. But, if the RAPs exceed the APs of time travelled, the Character has created a Nexus Event, and the changes are still in effect when s/he gets back to his or her own time.

To determine if the traveller arrived at the desired destination, roll an action check, Pushing the Character's INT. (That is, use the traveller's INT for both AV and OV. If the Character has Military Science/Tracking, s/he gets a -1 column shift to the RV.) Any positive RAPs indicate that the traveller recognizes his or her location.

30th Century Earth has erected a Time Beacon as a navigational aid for time travellers to locate their own timestream. Travellers who use the Beacon to return to the 30th Century get two column shifts to the left on their RV.

If the user, in his or her travels, dies or creates a situation in which s/he never existed, the Character encounters the Law of Death. The traveller ceases to exist in his or her own time, and other time travellers cannot go backward or forward to effect a rescue.

The actual process of time travel requires 0 APs.

Before the Crisis in the DC Comics universe, many alternate Earths existed. Most of the modern-day DC Characters inhabited Earth-1. After the Crisis, only Earth-1 remained.

The Pre-Crisis Earth-1 Superman is the most powerful incarnation of the Man of Steel. His physical strength is unmatched by any other hero. In fact, this Superman even surpasses his own counterparts: the 1940's Earth-2 Superman and the present-day Post-Crisis Man of Steel.

Even though Superman is a champion of Earth, he was born on the far-off planet of Krypton, a giant world orbiting an ancient red sun. The development of civilization on Krypton pre-dated the rise of the ancient cities of Earth by about 3,000 years. By the time of Krypton's destruction 40 years ago, its science technology was far more advanced than that of Earth's.

Shortly before the disaster, Krypton's leading scientist, Jor-El, found evidence of unstable elements in the planet's core. He knew that his world's destruction was imminent, but he could not convince Krypton's Science Council of these facts. Jor-El began work on a space ark in Kandor, only to have his plan fall through when the city was miniaturized and stolen by the Coluan android, Brainiac.

Shortly after Kandor's disappearance, Jor-El's wife Lara gave birth to a son, whom they named Kal-El. At the same time, Jor-El developed a projector which could send persons and objects into an other-dimensional "Phantom Zone." This was not the escape route for his people that he had hoped for. Instead, it was used as a prison for Krypton's criminals.

Jor-El turned his rescue efforts to rocketry. His co-worker, Jax-Ur, launched a rocket which destroyed one of Krypton's colonized moons, resulting in the Science Council's ban on space travel. Jor-El was forced to conduct any further rocket experiments in secret. He launched several test rockets, but he was not able to com lete a full-scale vehicle before Krypton went into its death-throes. Although there was room in the remaining test rocket for both their son Kal-El and Lara, Lara refused to leave her husband's side. The two watched as the rocket with their son lifted off. The rocket was bound for a planet known as Earth.

Moments later, Krypton dissolved in a final cataclysmic burst.

Travelling through a space warp, the rocket containing Kal-El crashed near the center of the North American continent. A childless, middle-aged couple, Jonathan and Martha Kent, were passing nearby as the capsule landed. When they investigated the site, they discovered the baby Kal-El. They were horrified at the inhumanity of what they thought was a space program experiment. The Clarks decided to secretly leave the child off at an orphanage, then return a few days later to apply for his adoption. The couple named the boy Clark. They discovered shortly

thereafter that the child possessed abilities far beyond those of any ordinary baby.

The Kents managed to keep their adopted son's powers a secret. As Clark grew older, Pa helped him develop his powers to their fullest. At the same time, Pa Kent took great pains to teach his adopted son the the virtues of Truth, Justice, and the American Way.

By the time Clark entered high school, he felt feel comfortable with his powers. Donning a colorful costume and taking the name of "Superboy," he began to fight crime and perform good deeds around his hometown of Smallville. He also obtained experience in concealing his secret identity from others.

After graduating from high school, Clark made plans to attend Metropolis University and major in Journalism. Before leaving for college, however, he suffered one of the greatest emotional blows of his life when Ma and Pa Kent died of an unknown fever. Swearing to uphold the ideals of his parents, Clark went to Metropolis University, where he graduated *magna cum laude.*

Upon graduation, Clark applied for a job at the Daily Planet. Despite his timid appearance, he was able to prove his worth to Perry White by turning in the first of what were to be many Superman headline stories.

Clark lead a double life as a hero and Daily Planet reporter for several years. During this Pre-Crisis period, Superman built his Fortress of Solitude in the Arctic wastes, helped to acclimate and train his cousin Kara (Supergirl) Zor-El, and became a charter member of the Justice League of America. He also met many of his major foes, such as the Parasite and Brainiac.

Recently, Galaxy Communications gained acquisition of the Daily Planet. Galaxy's owner, Morgan Edge, made Clark a roving reporter and, most recently, an anchorman for Galaxy's premiere TV station, WGBS.

EQUIPMENT:

SUPERMAN'S UNIFORM		
DEX: 0	STR: 0	BODY: 25
CHARGES: NA		
COST: 991 HPs + $ 350M		

POWERS:
Skin Armor: 10

SUPERBABY *alias Kal-El/Clark Kent*		
DEX: 13	STR: 36	BODY: 25
INT: 2	WILL: 6	MIND: 6
INFL: 3	AURA: 3	SPIRIT: 4
INITIATIVE: 18		HERO POINTS: 60

POWERS:
Directional Hearing: 10, Extended Hearing: 10, Flight: 27, Heat Vision: 20, Invulnerability: 31, Microscopic Vision: 10, Recall: 10, Sealed Systems: 20, Solar Sustenance: 50, Super Breath: 15, Super Hearing: 10, Superspeed: 15, Systemic Antidote: 10, Telescopic Vision: 10, X-Ray Vision: 15

LIMITATIONS:
Loses all Powers under red sun radiation.
X-Ray Vision can't penetrate lead.

VULNERABILITIES:

Rare Fatal and Loss:
Green Kryptonite: Range: 3

**Rare Miscellaneous:
(bizarre changes):**
Red Kryptonite: Range: 3

**Rare Miscellaneous Loss:
(permanent):**
Gold Kryptonite: Range: 3

Magic Miscellaneous:
all Powers, Skills, and Attributes against magic (Mystical Powers or objects) are at 4

Miscellaneous Loss:
Gravity attacks subtract their RAPs from all of Superbaby's Powers, Skills, and Attributes. No Power, Skill, or Attribute can be reduced to below zero.

MOTIVATION: NA
WEALTH: NA
JOB: NA
RACE: Normal Humanoid

EQUIPMENT:

SUPERBABY'S PLAYSUIT		
DEX: 0	STR: 0	BODY: 25
CHARGES: NA		
COST: 991 HPs + $ 350M		

POWERS:
Skin Armor: 10

SUPERBOY *alias Kal-El/Clark Kent*		
DEX: 24	STR: 47	BODY: 35
INT: 10	WILL: 16	MIND: 13
INFL: 7	AURA: 7	SPIRIT: 4
INITIATIVE: 41		HERO POINTS: 180

POWERS:
Directional Hearing: 10, Extended Hearing: 10, Flight: 44, Heat Vision: 28, Invulnerability: 43, Microscopic Vision: 15, Recall: 26, Sealed Systems: 20, Super Breath: 20, Super Hearing: 10, Superspeed: 24, Super Ventriloquism: 15, Systemic Antidote: 15, Telescopic Vision: 15, Thermal Vision: 15, X-Ray Vision: 20

SKILLS:
Charisma/Persuasion: 12, Gadgetry: 7, Scientist: 12, Scholar: 8 (All human languages, History)

LIMITATIONS:
• Loses all Powers under red sun radiation.
• X-Ray Vision can't penetrate lead.

VULNERABILITIES:
(All of Superboy's loss Vulnerabilities affect his Attributes, Powers, and Skills)

Rare Fatal and Loss:
Green Kryptonite: Range: 3

**Rare Miscellaneous:
(bizarre changes):**
Red Kryptonite: Range: 3

**Rare Miscellaneous Loss:
(permanent):**
Gold Kryptonite: Range: 3

Magic Miscellaneous:
all Powers, Skills, and attributes against magic (Mystical Powers or objects) are at 4.

Miscellaneous Loss:
Gravity attacks subtract their RAPs from all of Superboy's Powers, Skills, and attributes, but they cannot be reduced to below zero.

CONNECTIONS:
Smallville (high-level)
Smallville Penitentiary (high-level)
United Nations (low-level)
White House (low-level)

MOTIVATION: Upholding the Good
WEALTH: Comfortable
JOB: Student
RACE: Normal Humanoid

EQUIPMENT:

SUPERBOY'S UNIFORM		
DEX: 0	STR: 0	BODY: 25
CHARGES: NA		
COST: 991 HPs + $ 350M		

POWER:
Skin Armor: 10

PSYCHOLOGY

Superman, as the most famous powered hero of his adopted homeworld, has taken the role of Earth's champion upon himself. He not only fights crime, but also devotes his time to improving the good elements in the world. If all of the evil in the world vanished, Superman would still have a purpose to serve on Earth.

Superman has a great deal of respect for the Law. Even if he disagrees with a law he obeys it, trusting in the system to eventually correct any bad laws. He has made it a point to become a duly-deputized agent of the law in a number of countries.

Most important to Superman is the sanctity of all life. As he himself has said, "No one has the right to take a life. Not even Superman; especially not Superman." Several villains have tried to trick Superman into believing that he has taken a human life, knowing that this would mean the end of Superman's career.

Superman's uniqueness and separation from humanity has been a heavy burden over the years. His first true companionship came when Krypto, his pet dog, arrived on Earth. As Superman once explained, "...we could communicate in our own special way — through the shared experiences that were ours and ours alone! He was 'only' a dog ... but in some ways he was a closer friend to me than any other person on Earth!"

In later years he has developed more intellectually stimulating friendships with other heroes. He also helped to form the Justice League of America.

From time to time, Superman's powers make him overconfident to the point that he bites off more than he can chew. In the past, he felt that he must solve all of the problems of his adopted homeworld. He has, on numerous occasions, underestimated opponents; this sometimes resulted in dire consequences. In his first encounter with Mongul he played along with the villain's scheme and endangered countless billions of people, confident that he could beat Mongul and rescue his friends.

Superman has a private life as well. It is this side that he reveals when dealing with his closest friends: Lois Lane, Jimmy Olsen, Lana Lang, etc.

When Superman first met Lois, he kept himself at a professional distance despite her advances. During this time she spent a great of effort trying to determine his secret identity. As their friendship matured she gave up this pursuit, and Superman felt free to express his love for her. However, he thought that it would be unwise to marry her, as this would put her life in danger from his many enemies. Lois eventually grew tired of his fear of commitment and broke off their relationship. They are still friends, but Superman has yielded to Lois' desire to live her own life.

When Superman first met Jimmy Olsen, he saw him as a young friend whose insatiable curiosity often got him in trouble; this is why Superman gave him a signal watch. As Jimmy grew to become one of the Planet's top reporters, their relationship developed into a close friendship. Time and again, Jimmy has proven his courage and readiness to help his best pal. Superman will come to Jimmy for aid with situations in which he would trust no one else.

Since Supergirl came to Earth, Kal-El has been particularly close to her. At first, he treated her as a treasured student, then as a heroine in her own right. He is very proud of Kara but, more than that, he loves her as he would love a kid sister.

For a long time, Superman's closest friend was the Batman, who is a non-powered hero. His reason for fighting crime sometimes borders on the fanatical. Despite their differences, Superman and Batman worked well together because they represented the perfect melding of powers, skills, and intellect. Recently, the Batman has become dissatisfied with Superman's methods; the Batman's strong feelings on this matter have

driven a wedge between the two friends. Superman disagrees with his friend, but respects him nonetheless.

Clark Kent is a totally different aspect of Kal-El/Superman's personality. In fact, Clark Kent is almost a separate individual. Shortly after his first appearance as Superboy, Clark was instructed by Pa Kent, "You'll need more than a disguise, son. As Clark, you'll have to play a part, as if you were an actor. Make Clark everything Superboy ain't: mild-mannered, weak, and timid. In fact, you should disguise your voice when you're Clark and make it higher than Superboy's."

Clark took his father's advice to safeguard his dual identity, but the results of Clark's timidity have often caused him a great deal of pain. Running away from danger might have been an effective means for the teenaged Clark Kent to change to Superboy, but it branded him a coward and made him the butt of many jokes at Smallville High.

Clark has continued his mild-mannered ways to the present day. His reluctance to stand up for himself has not endeared him to many people. When danger threatens, Clark is usually nowhere to be found, having run away or pleaded a queasy spell. However, Clark will present a somewhat bolder front when he cannot get away to become Superman. His friends think that this is a hidden facet of his personality, and they try to encourage this boldness.

There are other exceptions to Clark's mild-mannered personality. Over the course of his many adventures, Clark has occasionally found himself bereft of Superman's powers. During these times, Clark Kent becomes more assertive. When he has no powers, he gradually allows his affection for Lois, his assertiveness towards Morgan Edge, and his resentment of Steve Lombard's bullying to surface. Invariably, however, his powers have returned and he reapplies his meek facade.

Clark's professional attitude is also bolder than his personal one. First as a reporter, then as a TV anchorman, he is cool and thoroughly professional. When meeting klutzy Kent for the first time, most people assume his professional demeanor is similar; they are often taken by surprise.

Both sides of Kal-El's personality are necessary. Without Clark Kent, Superman would lose his ability to interact with humans as individuals rather than as a homogeneous mass to be rescued. On the other hand, if Kal-El were "merely" Clark Kent, he would probably be desperately neurotic, perhaps braver, but always afraid to reveal his full potential.

METHODS

Superman has a wider range of powers than almost any other hero on Earth. Rather than depending on his high DEX and STR to engage his opponents in a slugfest with his opponents, he uses many different powers. He will often use his Super Breath and Heat Vision Powers rather than his high Physical Attributes. The only single attribute he wants to depent on is his intelligence.

Superman's powers are well-documented and his foes will regularly take his more flamboyant powers into account. As a result Superman has devised a large number of uses for his "lesser" Powers, such as his Vision and Hearing Powers. Perhaps Superman's greatest abilities, yet the qualities most often underrated, are his experience and intelligence.

Many of Superman's greatest opponents, such as Lex Luthor and Brainiac, have devised elaborate plans to get Superman out of the way while taking precautions against his powers. But, regardless of how intelligent or clever Superman's adversaries are, they invariably underestimate the Man of Tomorrow's keen wits.

For instance, Luthor once captured Superman and imprisoned him in a cell which bathed him in red sun radiation and high gravity, effectively negating his powers. Accustomed to thinking in scientific terms, Lex neglected to take into account the fact that Superman could hook the keys to the cell with his belt and escape.

Superman will *always* protect human life, innocent or not. He feels that he does not have the right to make life-and-death decisions for others. He will endanger himself or run the risk of letting the villain escape in order not to take a life, confident that he will survive the danger or capture the villain later. Even if his own death seems imminent, the Man of Steel will attempt to prevent the loss of human life. This often carries over into his dealings with allied heroes. For instance, he takes the brunt of attacks in battle alongside the Justice League.

Even in the heat of battle, Superman will find time to do productive deeds. For example, if he were sealed in a large chunk of ice, he would not only melt it with his Heat Vision, but he would do so over a drought-stricken community.

ROLE-PLAYING

Not all adventures require Armageddon-like battles. Superman should be given the chance to do good deeds. For example, if Metropolis was having a particularly warm winter, Superman might haul ice in from the North Pole to make a skating rink for young lovers and Olympic hopefuls. Superman's Subplots should provide chances for Superman's personality to shine forth; his vast Powers and Physical Attributes can sometimes overwhelm scenarios.

To encourage Players of the Superman Character to use all of his Powers as often as possible, we recommend that the Gamemaster award 15 Hero Points for each creative use for Superman's Powers other than simply slugging, frying, or blowing down an opponent, not to exceed a Standard Award for one adventure. The Gamemaster has the final say on what constitutes creative Power use.

NOTE: When designing adventures for Superman, the Gamemaster, like Superman's opponents, should not underestimate the Man of Tomorrow's abilities. His high APs put him on a level far above that of any other popular hero(ine). In creating a scenario for Superman, the Gamemaster should make sure that, using the "average roll of 15" rule from the *Gamemaster's Manual* (page 12), an opponent can damage Superman to the degree that the GM wishes. A good rule of thumb is that it takes 41-45 RAPs of Physical damage to do a minimum of damage to Superman (13 APs). It requires 66-70 RAPs to knock him unconscious.

SUPERMAN & MAGIC

On Krypton, the study and use of magic was rare. The genetic potential necessary to manipulate magical energies was even more rare in Kryptonians than it is in Earthlings. Since none of Superman's ancestors possessed such potential, he is vulnerable to magical forces (which are, in terms of game mechanics, Mystical attacks). Because most humans have some ancient ancestral magic background, they are much less vulnerable to magical attacks than Superman.

Superman's suit suffers a similar Vulnerability. Although Kryptonian materials under a yellow sun are resistant to many forms of attack, they offer no protection against Mystical attacks.

The question arises as to exactly when Superman's Attributes and Powers are reduced to 4 APs. Superman suffers this effect when:

1. He suffers any direct attack on his Mystical Attributes (Magic Blast, Spiritual Drain, Voodoo).

2. A Mystically Linked Power is directly used to create a situation which affects Superman. This could range from his being unable to see through a Mystically Linked Fog to being limited to 4 APs of Systemic Antidote against a Mystically Linked Poison Touch. This does *not* include indirect effects from the use of a Mystically Linked Power, such as a blow from an object through the use of a Mystically Linked Telekinesis Power.

3. Superman is directly effected by an object of Mystical origin (an Occultist object) or any creature of supernatural background, such as a vampire or werewolf.

4. The Mystical Powers of Animate Image, Lightning, Transmutation, Vampirism, and Weather Control are used against Superman by a character with mystic origins. A sorcerer with 7 APs of Lightning would get the benefit of Superman's reduced statistics; a Character like Cyborg would not.

To reflect Superman's Vulnerability, his Attributes are reduced to 4. However, to keep things simple, damage to Superman is subtracted from his normal current Attributes, with the following conditions:

1. Damage from Mystical Attacks on Mystical Attributes is deducted normally.

2. If Superman takes 4 or less APs of damage from Mystical attacks, the damage is subtracted from the appropriate current Resistance Attribute in the same manner as a normal attack.

3. If Superman takes 5 to 7 APs of damage from Mystical attacks on Physical or Mental Attributes, the current Resistance Attribute, unless already negative, is reduced to -1 and Superman is unconscious. If the current Attribute is already negative, it is then reduced to the negative of the Resistance Attribute.

4. If Superman takes 8 or more RAPs of damage from Mystical attacks on his Physical or Mental Attributes, the current Attribute is reduced to the negative of the Resistance Attribute.

It should be noted that these rules apply to any other Kryptonians currently known. If the Gamemaster decides to introduce a magic-using survivor of Krypton, such a Character will not suffer this Vulnerability.

LOIS LANE

DEX:	3	STR:	2	BODY:	2
INT:	3	WILL:	3	MIND:	2
INFL:	3	AURA:	2	SPIRIT:	2
INITIATIVE:	9 (13)	HERO POINTS:	15		

SKILLS:
Acrobatics/Climbing & Dodging: 2,
Artist/Writer: 4,
Charisma/Interrogation &
Persuasion: 3, Detective: 3, Martial
Arts/Attack Advantage & Taking a
Blow: 4, Thief/Locks and Safes &
Stealth: 3, Vehicles/Air, Land, and
Water: 2

MOTIVATION: Thrill of Adventure
WEALTH: Comfortable
JOB: Newspaper Reporter
RACE: Human

BACKGROUND

Lois was born on a farm near the
city of Pittsdale, the elder of Sam and
Ella Lane's two daughters. Her early
life was unexceptional. After graduating from Raleigh College, she
moved to Metropolis. She was determined to be the city's best reporter.

In short order, she began her job at
the Daily Planet as a city-beat reporter under editor Perry White. She
established herself as an outstanding
reporter due to her keen intelligence
and fierce determination.

Soon afterward, Superman came
to settle in Metropolis and made fast
friends with the staff of the Planet;
The Planet's reporters — especially
Lois — were eager to get super-
exclusives. After Superman rescued
Lois from a number of dangerous
situations, she became infatuated
with him and sought to persuade him
to marry her.

At seeming odds with her own
devotion to Superman and her disdain for Clark Kent, Lois tried time
and again to prove that the two men
were one and the same. She would
often place herself in great danger or
develop complicated ruses in order to
force Clark to reveal his secret identity. None of her schemes proved
conclusive.

Over the years, Lois matured. As
she ceased her childish games of
trying to prove Superman's secret
identity, she grew closer to Superman.
Eventually, she became known as
Superman's girlfriend.

Lois's fame as a newspaper
reporter spread; she earned awards
for excellence. Lois is now the Daily
Planet's top reporter and is assigned
to the most important stories.

A few years ago, Lois concluded
that Superman was not Clark Kent.
Her relationship with Clark soon
improved, and they are now close
friends.

Recently, Lois broke off her romantic involvement with Superman. She
felt that his protectiveness and reluc-

tance to expose her to danger had become smothering. Since then, no longer certain of super rescues, Lois is not quite as reckless.

PSYCHOLOGY

When Lois began her job as a reporter, she was daring as well as bright, and willing to risk any danger for a story. After she had grown accustomed to Superman's rescues, she became reckless, earning her the somewhat tongue-in-cheek title of "Bravest Woman in America." This phase eventually passed, much to Superman's relief. Newsgathering is very important to her, but she exercises reasonable caution in potentially dangerous situations.

When Lana Lang returned from Europe, Lois resented Lana's petty tricks to tarnish both Lois' reputation and her relationship with Superman. Lana's attitudes matured in short order, but the air between the two women is still cool.

Lois is friendly with Clark Kent. She considers him a shy man who is a trifle awkward, but brave when the situation demands it, and as committed to the responsibilities of journalism as she is.

Lois is no longer Superman's girlfriend, but she still has the utmost respect for who he is and what he stands for. Lois has repeatedly shown trust in Superman in situations where everyone else has abandoned him. She knows him better than anyone else, and she can see less obvious sides of his personality.

ROLE-PLAYING

Over the years, Lois has found herself in danger from several sources, especially from criminals she has gathered evidence against. Superman's foes have also attempted to use Lois as a hostage in order to blackmail Superman into overlooking their criminal activities. Fairly often, Lois has also been the victim of attempts to gain indirect vengeance against Superman through causing her injury or pain. At one point, Superman considered it a habit to rescue Lois.

Lois is more than capable of taking care of herself. Her quick thinking, bravery, and skill at the Kryptonian martial art of Klurkor allow her to get out of most scrapes herself.

JONATHAN KENT *Deceased*

DEX:	2	STR:	2	BODY:	2
INT:	2	WILL:	2	MIND:	3
INFL:	2	AURA:	2	SPIRIT:	2
INITIATIVE:		6	HERO POINTS:	5	

SKILLS:
Animal Handling: 2,
Charisma/Persuasion: 3,
Scholar/Academic Study
(Farming): 2, Vehicles/Land: 2

MOTIVATION: Upholding the Good
WEALTH: Comfortable
JOB: Farmer, Grocer
RACE: Human

MARTHA KENT (CLARK) *Deceased*

DEX:	2	STR:	2	BODY:	2
INT:	2	WILL:	3	MIND:	2
INFL:	2	AURA:	2	SPIRIT:	2
INITIATIVE:		6	HERO POINTS:	0	

SKILLS:
Scholar/Academic Study
(Cooking): 2

MOTIVATION: Upholding the Good
WEALTH: Comfortable
JOB: Farmer
RACE: Human

Jonathan and Martha Kent are the two most important individuals in Superman's life. They instilled in him the virtues which make him the hero he is today.

BACKGROUND

Although little is known of Martha Kent's background, her husband, Jonathan Kent, was born of farmers in the Midwest. When Jonathan married Martha they moved to a farm outside of Smallville.

Married for many years, the couple had no children. They were well into middle-age when, driving past a field one fateful day, they saw a rocket crash to the ground. They investigated the rocket and found an infant boy. Believing the boy to be the victim of some sinister space-program experiment, they decided to claim him as their own. Jonathan and Martha left him at the doorstep of the local orphanage, and returned several days later to legally adopt him. They chose Martha's maiden name of Clark for the child's first name.

It was not long before they discovered that Clark possessed many incredible abilities. The Kents realized that Clark was intended for some great destiny, and they trained him as best they could. Afraid that the child's powers would frighten others, or that unscrupulous individuals would exploit his powers for evil purposes, they kept Clark's powers secret.

Eventually they sold the farm, moved into Smallville, and started a small grocery store which prospered. Clark attended Smallville High and served as Superboy in his spare time. In several encounters with other surviving Kryptonians, Clark eventually discovered his Kryptonian heritage.

While Jonathan and Martha were on a Caribbean vacation after Clark's graduation, they caught a rare fever. Despite his best efforts, Clark could find no cure, and he was forced to wait at his foster parents' deathbeds, witnessing his mother's death. Jonathan slipped away shortly thereafter, but not before he made Clark promise to use his powers for the good of humanity.

PSYCHOLOGY

Despite their lack of experience in raising children, Jonathan and Martha Kent rose to the occasion admirably. They treated Clark as they would treat a natural-born son.

Ever since Clark told his adoptive parents about his Kryptonian parents, Jonathan had became somewhat insecure about the fact that Clark's true father was a famous scientist with many incredible achievements. However, he was the father that Jor-El was unable to be to Clark/Kal-El. Martha was an endless font of love for her foster son.

ROLE-PLAYING

In any adventure which takes place during Superboy's time, Ma and Pa Kent should stand as the ideal parents. They always provide support, understanding, love, and care for Clark. They are sure to make him realize the correct course he should select, but they always let him make final decisions regarding his responsibilities himself.

JAMES BARTHOLEMEW (Jimmy) OLSEN

DEX:	4	STR:	2	BODY:	3
INT:	2	WILL:	2	MIND:	2
INFL:	2	AURA:	2	SPIRIT:	2
INITIATIVE:	8	HERO POINTS:	20		

POWERS:

Stretching: 5

SKILLS:

Artist/Photographer & Writer: 3,
Charisma/Interrogation: 2,
Detective: 2, Vehicles/Air &
Land: 2

LIMITATIONS:

Stretching Power requires drinking
a potion, which takes effect on the
phase after imbibing it. Power lasts
for 1D10 hours.

MOTIVATION: Thrill of Adventure
WEALTH: Comfortable
JOB: Reporter
RACE: Human

EQUIPMENT:

LEGION FLIGHT RING

DEX:	0	STR:	4	BODY:	5
INT:	0	WILL:	0	MIND:	0
CHARGES:	45				
COST:	10,321 HPs + $ 7.9Q				

POWERS:

Flight: 8, Super Ventriloquism
(limited signalling capability): 62

SIGNAL WATCH

DEX:	0	STR:	0	BODY:	2
INT:	0	WILL:	0	MIND:	0
CHARGES:	20				
COST:	608 HPs + $ 260M				

POWERS:

Super Ventriloquism (Signalling
Only): 24

BACKGROUND

Jimmy Olsen was barely in his teens
when he began working for the Daily
Planet as an office boy. During one
"Boys' Day" in Metropolis, he took
over the editor's desk and did an
excellent job. When Jimmy turned 16,
he advanced to the position of cub
reporter and photographer.

Like Lois, Jimmy found his eager-
ness and curiosity leading him into
danger at times. Superman, con-
cerned about his young friend's wel-
fare, constructed a signal watch with
which Jimmy could call him in an
emergency. When activated, the
watch would emit an ultra-sonic
signal which Superman could hear
even at great distances.

Many people saw a similarity
between the Superman/Jimmy Olsen
and the Batman/Robin duos. Sometimes Jimmy and Robin would team
up to assist their elders as a separate
team. Jimmy and Superman occasionally teamed up as a duo known as
Nightwing and Flamebird.

Jimmy also had a hero career of his
own. He initially gained his Stretching
Power from an alien artifact. Kryptonite radiation cost him this power,
but a special serum created by Professor Potter allowed him to regain it
for hours at a time. He called himself
Elastic Kid and occasionally fought
crime. His courage and resourceful-
ness earned him a reserve membership in the Legion of Super-Heroes.
He rarely becomes Elastic Kid or
teams up with the Legion these days.

After he graduated from Metropolis High, Jimmy earned a promotion
to full-time reporter at the Daily
Planet. He assumed many of Clark
Kent's old responsibilities, and
quickly established himself as a
superb reporter who was nearly on a
par with Clark and Lois Lane.

PSYCHOLOGY

Jimmy is consistently underrated
due to his young age and his association with journalists of greater fame.
However, his association with these
journalists works to his advantage; he
has many opportunities to learn from
his more experienced colleagues.
Also, his quick wits and bravery
enable him to get out of danger.

Jimmy's bravery is second to none.
Unlike Lois, Jimmy does not depend
on Superman to rescue him. He has
stood at Superman's side many times
against villains far more powerful
than himself. However, he is not
reckless by any means. With his signal
watch he knows he can count on
Superman to get him out of a jam, but
he always takes reasonable precautions and tries to avoid involving
Superman in situations that he can
get out of on his own. Unlike Lois and
Lana, Jimmy has never taken his
special relationship with the Man of
Steel for granted.

Although Jimmy's relationship
with Clark and Lois is a long-standing

one, he is not particularly close to
either of them. Over the years, his
friendship with Superman has
matured from simple hero-worship
to a mutual respect and affection. He
feels that being Superman's pal
carries a great deal of responsibility;
he has shown himself to be up to the
task time and again.

ROLE-PLAYING

Even though Jimmy has a Signal
Watch, he is not always the prime
candidate for a villain to use against
Superman. Any one of Superman's
friends could be chosen for that.

Jimmy is portrayed as a confidante
and as an assistant to his best friend.
His ingenuity and courage lead him
into situations that a clever Gamemaster can take advantage of.

LIMITATIONS:
The Bio-Ring only allows Lana to Shape Change into insect or anthropoid forms. She can only use the same form once in 24 hours and retains human size. Only the lower half of her body Shape Changes.

MOTIVATION: Thrill of Adventure
WEALTH: Affluent
JOB: Anchorwoman
RACE: Human
EQUIPMENT:

BIO-GENETIC RING		
DEX: 0 STR: 0 BODY: 3		
CHARGES: 74		
COST: 74 HPs + $ 11K		

POWERS:
Shape Change: 7

BACKGROUND

Lana Lang was the daughter of Professor Lewis Lang, a noted archaeologist living in semi-retirement in Smallville. Lana was a bright and outgoing teenager who befriended her mild-mannered classmate Clark Kent. Their relationship was a strong one. At times Lana would act kindly towards Clark, but she would then turn around and berate him for his seeming cowardice.

The root of Lana's confusion might lie in her conviction that Clark was secretly Superboy. Lana entertained herself for hours with schemes to prove that Clark had indestructible hair or Superboy's fingerprints. None of her ruses succeeded, but she did not tire of trying for many years.

An interesting facet of Lana's past is her career as Insect Queen. An alien acquaintance gave Lana a bio-genetic ring, which bestowed upon her the ability to assume the powers and physical form of any insect. This power, coupled with the courage and kindness which she learned from the experience of having the ring, merited a Reserve Membership in the Legion of Super-Heroes. As she grew older, Lana found this ability disquieting and has not used it in recent years.

After high school and a short stint as a reporter for WMET-TV in Metropolis, Lana took an extended trip to Europe. There she married and had a child, but the child was killed by terrorists. She then divorced her husband and returned to Metropolis.

In Metropolis, WGBS hired Lana to be Clark's co-anchor. Although she said nothing about what had happened in Europe, her colleagues who knew her before the tragedy of her child's death could see that she had changed. She was vain and condescending. She even began a predatory campaign to steal Superman away from Lois.

After seeing some of her actions mirrored by the possessive love of the Master Jailer and receiving a stern lecture from Superman, Lana realized what she was doing and took steps to make amends.

When Vartox once appeared on Earth, he and Lana fell in love. It is a hopeless romance, but Lana has promised to wait for him.

PSYCHOLOGY

In high school, Lana was spunky and bright. Her yearbook called her the class wit. She liked Clark and tried to get him to show more backbone, but she pined for Superboy.

As she grew, Lana developed great courage. When aliens threatened to destroy Earth unless Superman would directly take a life, Lana was willing to commit suicide so that Superman could claim he killed her.

The loss of her child in Europe devastated her. When she returned to Metropolis, she hid her pain behind snooty attitudes and mannerisms. Lana has dropped most of her condescending habits as time dulled the grief she felt over the death of her child.

As brave as she is, Lana is a bit on the flighty side. Lois has said that Lana has the sensitivity of a brick.

ROLE-PLAYING

Lana has claimed to be a friend of Superman. This is a hazard as well as an honor. Repeatedly, she has found herself in peril from those with a grudge against the Man of Steel.

In addition, her father has become something of an expert at investigating lost civilizations or sealed tombs. More than once, Professor Lang has required Superman's assistance with an unearthed menace.

LANA LANG		
DEX: 4	STR: 2	BODY: 2
INT: 2	WILL: 2	MIND: 2
INFL: 2	AURA: 2	SPIRIT: 2
INITIATIVE: 8		HERO POINTS: 10

SKILLS:
Artist/Acting: 2,
Charisma/Persuasion: 3,
Scholar/Linguistics
(European 2): 2, Thief/Stealth: 2,
Vehicles/Air & Land: 2

PETE ROSS

DEX:	3	STR:	2	BODY:	2
INT:	2	WILL:	2	MIND:	2
INFL:	2	AURA:	2	SPIRIT:	2
INITIATIVE:	7		HERO POINTS:		5

SKILLS (as an adult):
Scholar/Academic Study
(Engineering, Geology): 3
WEALTH: Affluent
JOB: Engineer
RACE: Human

JON ROSS

DEX:	2	STR:	1	BODY:	2
INT:	2	WILL:	2	MIND:	2
INFL:	2	AURA:	2	SPIRIT:	2
INITIATIVE:	6		HERO POINTS:		5

SKILLS:
Military Science: 3,
Scholar/Academic Study (Military
Tactics): 3, Weaponry: 2
WEALTH: Affluent
JOB: Student
RACE: Human

BACKGROUND

Pete Ross, a Smallville native, was a school friend of Clark Kent. One night, several of the high-school boys were camping when a thunderstorm came up. During the storm, Clark changed to Superboy and flew off to attend to a matter that required his attention. Pete was awake later than anyone else and saw Clark change into Superboy in the light of a lightning bolt.

Pete, being a true friend, told no one of his discovery. Pete did not let Clark know that he knew about the dual identity because he did not want Clark to worry about his safety.

Pete used this knowledge to save Superboy's life on a couple of occasions. He once filled in for Superboy when Clark was suffering from amnesia. The Legion of Super-Heroes made Pete an honorary member in recognition of his importance to Superboy. Superboy had been a member of the Legion of Super-Heroes since receiving a special membership that would permit him to continue to live in the 20th Century and visit the Legion in the 30th Century when he chose to.

Pete grew up and became a successful geologist and an engineer. He married and had a son, Jon. Divorced under unrevealed circumstances.

Pete got custody of Jon and then moved to Metropolis.

Clark often watched Jon when Pete was busy, and the two became fast friends. Jon eventually learned of Superman's dual identity. As his father had done, Jon proved his friendship to Superman by using his knowledge of the secret identity several times to save Superman's life.

The Ross' situation took a bizarre turn when an alien race from the planet Nyrvn kidnapped Jon. Even though the Nyrvnians were expert technicians, they needed to kidnap aliens from other planets who had an aptitude for appropriate military skills, as their race had a mental block against learning such abilities. They chose to kidnap young Jon Ross because they somehow believed that Jon possessed an inborn talent for the military sciences.

Pete revealed his knowledge of Superman's identity to Clark Kent and asked him to rescue Jon. The Man of Tomorrow attempted to do so, only to discover that Jon's talents were necessary to the Nyrvnians' survival.

Driven nearly insane by the loss of his son, Pete used equipment he found at one of Luthor's abandoned lairs to pull Superboy forward in time and then switch minds. His mind in Superboy's body negated the law of time travel, which prevents the existence of the same two persons at the same point in time. Pete attempted to kill Superman, but was ultimately defeated.

Pete was committed to an asylum. The guilt that Superman felt at failing his old friend was used as a focus for a Mystical attack by Talia, Queen of Darkness. The mysterious Phantom Stranger defeated Talia before she could complete the spell, and Superman was able to rescue Jon from the Nyrvnians. Pete and Jon were reunited after the ordeal and have since moved back to Smallville.

ROLE-PLAYING

During Clark's teen years, Pete was his closest friend. He often stepped in to help when Superboy was threatened, often "accidentally" helping to cover Clark's secret identity.

As an adult, Pete suffered the burdens of keeping such a secret. He was briefly insane while Jon was with the Nyrvnians, and his perceived failure as a husband has left great scars on his psyche.

Jon Ross has a child's faith in Superman's ability to rise above any situation, and will help the Man of Steel whenever possible.

PERRY WHITE

DEX:	2	STR:	2	BODY:	2
INT:	3	WILL:	2	MIND:	2
INFL:	3	AURA:	2	SPIRIT:	3
INITIATIVE:	8			HERO POINTS:	0

SKILLS:
  Artist/Writer: 2,
  Charisma/Persuasion: 2,
  Scholar/Academic Study
  (Journalistic History): 2,
  Thief/Stealth: 1

WEALTH: Comfortable
JOB: Newspaper Editor
RACE: Human

EQUIPMENT:

SUPER CIGAR

DEX:	0	STR:	0	BODY:	1
INT:	0	WILL:	0	MIND:	0
CHARGES:	8				
COST:	2189 HPs + $ 7.2B				

POWERS:
Adaptation: 35

LIMITATION:
  Adaptation can only be used to
  gain Physical Attributes and
  Powers.
  White must smoke entire Super
  Cigar to gain Adaptation Power.

BACKGROUND

Perry White began working for the Daily Planet as a newsboy in the 1930's. His journalistic drive was such that one of his first assignments as a reporter was war correspondent during World War II.

Perry was known in his day for his investigative zeal. His hard-hitting stories regularly put ganglords in prison. When he took George Taylor's position as Planet editor, he continued his diligence in his work and encouraged the same kind of dedication in his reporters.

White built the Planet into a world-famous model of tough, but ethical, investigative journalism. For this, he was awarded several prizes, including three Pulitzers.

At one point, Perry helped Superman free a civilization of mutant teens from the hypnotic control of the tyrant Calixto. In gratitude, the mutants gave Perry a box of "super cigars" which would give him the ability to acquire the Physical attributes and Powers of other Characters. He has one cigar left; it is locked in a wall-safe in his office for a future emergency.

Perry and his wife have had a difficult marriage of late, but they are making an effort to reconcile.

Perry is rarely involved in Superman's adventures. He is seldom seen outside the Daily Planet offices and spends most of his time working on his newspaper.

PROFESSOR PHINEAS POTTER				
Dex:	2	Str:	2	Body:	2
Int:	5	Will:	2	Mind:	4
Infl:	3	Aura:	2	Spirit:	2
Initiative:	10	Hero Points:	5		

SKILLS:
Gadgetry: 6, Scholar: 6 (all scientific fields), Scientist: 10
WEALTH: Affluent
JOB: Amateur Inventor
RACE: Human

BACKGROUND

Professor Potter, Lana Lang's uncle, is a brilliant, yet eccentric scientist. During Clark's career as Superboy, the Professor invented many bizarre items while living on the outskirts of Smallville. Although inarguably brilliant, the professor is easily distracted and somewhat eccentric.

Most of his Smallville inventions were impressive but useless items, such as a machine that can squeeze 2,000 gallons of onion juice per hour! Every so often, one of his weird creations would go awry and require Superboy's attention.

When Lana went to Metropolis after graduating, her uncle followed — half to keep an eye on her and half to benefit from Metropolis' impressive scientific faculties.

PSYCHOLOGY

Professor Potter is a quiet and likable old man; he is actually delightful in his apparent absent-mindedness. He is helpful to anyone in need; this has proven inconvenient for

Superman when Lois and Lana enlisted Potter's aid to attempt to penetrate the secret of the Man of Tomorrow's duel identity.

Professor Potter has also assisted Superman on a few occasions, such as the time he deduced that the antidote for a particular isotope of Red Kryptonite consisted of large doses of certain acids. He also helped Superman repair an inter-dimensional transport mechanism.

ROLE-PLAYING

Potter can be used to set up a number of scenarios. He can invent something that functions other than as planned, requiring Superman's attention. He might also need Superman's assistance to complete some experiment.

MORGAN EDGE				
Dex:	2	Str:	2	Body:	2
Int:	3	Will:	2	Mind:	3
Infl:	3	Aura:	2	Spirit:	2
Initiative:	8	Hero Points:	0		

SKILLS:
Charisma/Intimidation: 4, Scholar/Academic Study (Business): 3
WEALTH: Multimillionaire
JOB:
President of Galaxy Corporations
RACE: Human

BACKGROUND

Morgan Edge became the president of Galaxy Communications by taking a hand in matters that many executives ignore. When the company bought the Daily Planet, he continued that practice by making some personnel changes.

Convinced that a popular reporter like Clark Kent could add prestige to Galaxy's flagship affiliate, WGBS-TV, Edge reassigned Kent to the evening news as anchorman. Since then he has taken a direct hand many times, such as when he assigned Kent to write the story of Superman's ancestry as a novel-length best-seller.

PSYCHOLOGY

Edge is a strict task-master. He will bully an employee if he feels like it, and will allow no dissension. He is usually right with his hunches, and his fortune continues to grow.

ROLE-PLAYING

Morgan Edge rarely gets involved in Superman's adventures. He is best used in a Workplace Subplot. He may give Clark a special rating-grabbing assignment, but he rarely requires Superman to save him.

Morgan is a tyrannical employer. He would doubtless have a high employee turnover rate if not for two things: he is always right, and he pays extremely well.

STEVE LOMBARD				
Dex:	3	Str:	3	Body:	3
Int:	2	Will:	3	Mind:	3
Infl:	2	Aura:	2	Spirit:	2
Initiative:	7 (10)	Hero Points:	15		

SKILLS:
Acrobatics/Dodging: 3, Artist/Actor: 2, Martial Artist/Attack Advantage: 3, Vehicles/Land: 2
WEALTH: Affluent
JOB: Sporting Goods Store Owner
RACE: Human

BACKGROUND

Steve Lombard began his public career playing football for the Metropolis Meteors. He was involved in a cheating scandal over illegal drugs and quit the team. He was hired by WGBS-TV as a sportscaster.

Steve is competent at his job but, unlike Clark, Steve is not a team player. A bully in high school, Steve has changed little. He has made it a regular practice to trip Clark when he is carrying a tray of food in the employee's cafeteria, or splash him with a puddle while speeding by in his expensive sports car. Mysteriously, many of these pranks go awry, making Steve, not Clark, look foolish.

Months ago, when Galaxy was in dire financial straits, the station had to lay Steve off. This has engendered a maturity never before seen in the big guy. When Clark lost his job due to a plot by Lex Luthor, Steve was understanding and supportive.

ROLE-PLAYING

Steve is still athletic. His jocular arrogance, his reputation as a member of Superman's circle of friends, and his physical overconfidence might generate many plots for Superman.

SKILLS:

Artist/Actor: 7,
Charisma/Persuasion: 18,
Detective: 7, Scholar: 10 (All
human languages, Literature,
Psychology, History, Scientist)

LIMITATIONS:

Loses all Powers under red sun
radiation

VULNERABILITIES:

*(All of Supergirl's loss
Vulnerabilities affect her
attributes, Powers, and Skills)*

**Rare, Fatal and Loss
Vulnerabilities:**
Green Kryptonite: Range: 3
**Rare Miscellaneous Loss
(permanent):**
Gold Kryptonite: Range: 3
**Rare Miscellaneous (bizarre
changes):**
Red Kryptonite: Range: 3
Magic Miscellaneous:
All attributes, Powers and Skills
against magic (Mystical Powers or
objects) are at 4 APs.
Miscellaneous Loss:
Gravity Attacks subtract their
RAPs from all of Supergirl's
attributes, Powers, and Skills, but
these cannot be reduced below
zero.

CONNECTIONS:

City of Chicago (low-level)
Press (high-level)
United Nations (high-level)
Justice League of America
(high-level)
White House (high-level)

MOTIVATION: Upholding the Good
WEALTH: Affluent
JOB: Student, Camera Crewman,
Guidance Counsellor, Soap Opera
Actress
RACE: Normal Humanoid
EQUIPMENT:

Supergirl is the younger cousin of
Kal-El and a heroine in her own right.
Over the years she has established
herself as one of the best crimefight-
ers on Earth, on a par with Superman.

BACKGROUND

Kara is the daughter of Zor-El, the
greatest scientist of Argo City. Before
the destruction of Krypton, Zor-El
covered the city with a weatherproof
plastic dome. When the planet
exploded, the city, which was still
intact, was flung out into space. The
same reaction that converted por-
tions of the planet Krypton into Green
Kryptonite also affected the area of
Krypton in which Argo City was
located, but the inhabitants covered
it with lead to shield them from any
adverse effects.

During Argo City's voyage through
space, Zor-El married Alura In-Ze;
they had a daughter whom they
named Kara. When Kara was fifteen,
a meteor storm ripped open Argo
City's lead shielding. Zor-El constructed a spaceship to rocket his
daughter to safety. At the same time,
Alura, searching for a refuge for Kara,
discovered Earth and learned of
Superman and his Kryptonian origins. After making a costume for Kara
similar to Superman's, the couple
rocketed their daughter to Earth.

Kara arrived on Earth and confronted Superman with their family
relationship. Superman took her to
Midvale Orphanage to give her time
to adjust to life on Earth and perfect
her powers in private. She secretly
performed heroics on several occasions, joined the Legion of Super-
Heroes, and eventually proved herself
worthy as a powered heroine. She
was adopted by Fred and Edna
Danvers and given the name of Linda
Lee. She eventually revealed to her
adoptive parents and the world that
she was Supergirl.

After graduating from Midvale
High, Kara went to Stanhope University. After graduation she worked at a
TV station in San Francisco. She then
fluctuated between a student advisor
job, post-grad work, and an acting
role on a soap opera. She was a part-
time heroine on many occasions, but
she eventually went back to college at
Lakeshore University in Chicago.

SUPERGIRL *alias Kara Zor-El—Deceased*		
DEX: 26	STR: 48	BODY: 36
INT: 13	WILL: 19	MIND: 13
INFL: 10	AURA: 8	SPIRIT: 4
INITIATIVE: 49	HERO POINTS: 150	

POWERS:

Directional Hearing: 10, Extended
Hearing: 10, Flight: 45, Heat
Vision: 28, Invulnerability: 45,
Microscopic Vision: 15, Recall: 28,
Sealed Systems: 20, Solar
Sustenance: 50, Super Breath: 20,
Super Hearing: 10, Superspeed: 24,
Super Ventriloquism: 15, Systemic
Antidote: 15, Telescopic Vision: 15,
Thermal Vision: 15, X-Ray
Vision: 20

SUPER UNIFORM		
DEX: 0	STR: 0	BODY: 20
CHARGES: NA		
COST: 631 HPs + $ 30M		

POWERS:
Skin Armor: 10

She was eventually reunited with her true parents, who had escaped into the Survival Zone, a dimension similar to the Phantom Zone. They escaped and went to live in Kandor.

During the Crisis, Supergirl was killed at the hands of the Anti-Monitor; she sacrificed her life to save her adopted world.

PSYCHOLOGY

Influenced by her famous cousin and determined to uphold the honor of Krypton, Kara has matured from a bubbly, cheerful teen to an affable, yet determined young woman. Like Superman and many others who Uphold the Good, she performs many more good deeds than just fighting criminals and powered villains. Her determination is second to none. However, when aroused, her ferocity is almost frightening in its intensity.

In comparison to Kal-El, Kara has a somewhat more optimistic outlook on life. She is more willing to believe in the inherent good of the world; she has not encountered as many ruthless villains (like Luthor or Brainiac) as her cousin.

ROLE-PLAYING

In combat, Supergirl's abilities make her a formidable opponent. Although she is not as experienced as Superman, she is well acquainted with her powers and is rarely taken off-guard.

In her personal life, Kara is easygoing and likable, with many friends and acquaintances. Her fluctuating employment situation is the result of uncertainty about her adopted lifestyle, not personal indecision.

AMBUSH BUG *alias Irwin Schwab*

DEX:	6	STR:	2	BODY:	3
INT:	3	WILL:	3	MIND:	3
INFL:	5	AURA:	4	SPIRIT:	4
INITIATIVE:		14 * HERO POINTS:		180	

* SPECIAL: The APs of his suit's Teleportation are added to Ambush Bug's Initiative when he is teleporting. With the use of Hero Points, Ambush Bug can boost his suit's Teleportation Power to 46 APs, making his effective Initiative 60.

POWERS:

Dumb Luck: 15, Reality Check: 12

SKILLS:

Scholar/Academic Study (DC Universe lore, bad TV shows): 9

MOTIVATION: Thrill of Adventure
WEALTH: Struggling
JOB: Hero for Hire
RACE: Human
EQUIPMENT:

SUIT

DEX:	0	STR:	0	BODY:	25
INT:	0	WILL:	0	MIND:	0
CHARGES:	NA				
COST:	2650 HPs + $ 7.8B				

POWERS:

Invulnerability: 30,
Teleportation: 23

NOTE: The suit will eat anyone other than Irwin who attempts to wear it. Treat this as a Cell Rot attack of 12 APs.

BACKGROUND

Little is known of the man who calls himself "Ambush Bug." This hero-for-hire has fought several menaces in defense of Metropolis, and is sometimes an ally of Superman.

On the other hand, much is known of the origins of Irwin Schwab and his amazing Teleportation suit. Unfortunately, it's all extremely contradictory and confusing, so we won't try to explain it here.

Ambush Bug's debut was as a villain (of sorts). His first appearance was during a Metropolis Day parade, when he seemed to have killed District Attorney Syms. The Bug was also pursuing an ill-fated love affair with Negative Woman of the Doom Patrol at that time. He was captured by Superman and imprisoned, but the murder charges were dropped (DA Syms got better) and he escaped shortly thereafter.

Ambush Bug was accidentally taken to the 30th Century by Superman, where he was temporarily left with the Legion of Substitute Heroes. Now less a villain than a fun-loving trickster, the Bug bounced around 30th-Century Metropolis until he was tricked into the Phantom Zone. Superman considered leaving him there, but decided that was too cruel a fate for the Phantom Zoners, so the Man of Steel removed Irwin and returned him to his proper time.

Ambush Bug decided to become a hero. He went to Chicago to fight crime alongside the valiant Supergirl. Despite his protestations of turning over a new leaf, branching out into the hero biz, and rooting out crime down to its bitter tubers, Ambush Bug was taken to Arkham Asylum. He was soon let out by a unanimous vote of the board of directors.

Irwin took up heroing for real, started a storefront detective agency, and promptly discovered Superman's secret ID. After several false starts (including an unfortunate incident with the big red "S," a piece of Red Kryptonite and a terribly confused Kobra) the Bug won a name for himself after defeating Quantis, the Koala who walks like a man, and a squad of Republican terrorists.

Since then, there have been repeated rumors of the Bug's demise at the hands (or feet) of kamikaze killer socks (you don't want to know) and a possible eviction from the DC universe. It is unlikely that this will keep Ambush Bug down; he will undoubtedly return to aid Superman in the battle for Truth, Justice, and the American Way.

PSYCHOLOGY

That's a hard one. Ambush Bug is either A) a loon, B) a loon who thinks he's a sane man, C) a sane man who thinks he's a loon, or D) none of the above. To put it in the most charitable terms possible, Ambush Bug is an expert tactician who uses bad puns, poor jokes, and a facade of insanity to keep his opponents guessing. [Sure.]

ROLE-PLAYING

Ambush Bug is fun. Trust us. He is best used as a foil for the unflappable Man of Tomorrow. His lunacy is such that he might revert back to the fun-loving trickster of yesteryear, or attempt to assist Superman with the best of intentions, feeling that Supes can't get along without him.

The best way to appreciate Ambush Bug's unfailing ability to liven up a scenario is to read *Ambush Bug, Son of Ambush Bug, DC Comics Presents #52, #59 and #81*, or our *Don't Ask!* adventure, by Scott Jenkins.

LIMITATIONS:
Loses all Powers under red sun radiation
Physical and Mental limitations of a normal dog
X-Ray Vision cannot penetrate lead

VULNERABILITIES:
(All of Krypto's loss Vulnerabilities affect his Attributes, Powers, and Skills)
Rare, Fatal and Loss Vulnerabilities:
Green Kryptonite: Range: 3
Rare Miscellaneous Loss (permanent):
Gold Kryptonite: Range: 3
Rare Miscellaneous (bizarre changes):
Red Kryptonite: Range: 3
Magic Miscellaneous:
All attributes, Powers, and Skills against magic (Mystical Powers or objects) are at 4 APs.
Miscellaneous Loss:
Gravity Attacks subtract their RAPs from all of Krypto's attributes, Powers, and Skills, but these cannot be reduced to less than zero.

MOTIVATION: Thrill of Adventure
WEALTH: NA
JOB: NA
RACE: Animal (Kryptonese dog)

Krypto is the loyal pet of Superboy and, later, Superman. He has aided his master on many occasions.

BACKGROUND

Although Krypto was originally bought by Jor-El as a pet for his child, Jor-El was forced to use the dog in one of his rocket experiments. Krypto was successfully launched into orbit, but a meteor collision knocked the rocket off into space. When Krypton exploded 58 days later, Krypto's capsule was drawn to Earth through the same space-warp as Kal-El's escape craft.

Unable to break out of the indestructible craft, Krypto was captive until the rocket crashed on Earth. The dog then tracked Clark Kent/Superboy down to Smallville and led him back to the rocket, where Super-

KRYPTO		
DEX: 24	STR: 44	BODY: 35
INT: 1	WILL: 7	MIND: 8
INFL: 4	AURA: 3	SPIRIT: 4
INITIATIVE: 29	HERO POINTS: 80	

POWERS:
Analytical Smell/Tracking Scent: 15, Directional Hearing: 10, Empathy: 10, Extended Hearing: 10, Flight: 43, Invulnerability: 43, Microscopic Vision: 15, Sealed Systems: 20, Solar Sustenance: 50, Super Breath: 20, Super Hearing: 12, Superspeed: 24, Systemic Antidote: 20, Telescopic Vision: 15, Thermal Vision: 15, X-Ray Vision: 20

SKILLS:
Charisma/Intimidation: 13, Military Science/Tracking: 8

boy discovered the dog's origins.

Krypto often assisted his young master, disguising himself as Chip, Clark's pet, with the aid of a wood-stain dark patch.

Krypto eventually left Earth, but returned to Superman years later, old and in poor shape. Superman sent Krypto to a "fountain of youth" that rejuvenated the dog and made him temporarily immune to the Kryptonite meteors that surrounded the Earth. Krypto set out from Earth, built a Doghouse of Solitude, and has only returned for brief visits since.

PSYCHOLOGY

Although Krypto's intelligence is as far above an ordinary dog's as Superman's is above a human, he is still basically a dog, and acts accordingly. He is playful and usually cheerful, but can become extremely menacing when anything threatens his master. His animal instincts allow him to detect thoughts of hate and fear and he can usually penetrate the disguises of criminals.

ROLE-PLAYING

Krypto should be treated exactly as a dog. He rarely uses his powers in unique and unusual ways. His attention span is fairly limited and he can often be distracted by things that would not distract a human.

LORI LEMARIS *Deceased*

DEX:	6	STR:	3	BODY:	5
INT:	6	WILL:	4	MIND:	5
INFL:	4	AURA:	4	SPIRIT:	3
INITIATIVE:	16	HERO POINTS:	45		

POWERS:
Empathy: 4, Swimming: 7, Ultra Vision: 8, Water Freedom: 8, Telepathy: 8

SKILLS:
Acrobatics/Diving: 4, Charisma: 3, Scholar/Academic Study (Undersea Lore): 5

LIMITATIONS:
Lori is a mermaid and is unable to do anything requiring two legs.

Empathy only works on marine life.

Lori must immerse herself in water every hour. If she spends more time out of water, she begins to die as per the Fatal Vulnerability rules.

MOTIVATION: Upholding the Good
WEALTH: Affluent
JOB: None
RACE: Exotic Humanoid

Lori Lemaris was one of the great loves of Superman's life, although more recently she became just a close friend.

BACKGROUND

Lori was a resident of the Atlantean city of Tritonis and, like all of the Tritonians, was mutated into a mer-person by the serum they took to survive the submerging of Atlantis.

Chosen by her people to visit the surface world, Lori attended Metropolis University, where she met and fell in love with Clark Kent. Clark reciprocated the feelings and offered to give up his secret identity to marry her, but she felt the marriage between the two dissimilar races was hopeless and declined. Years later, the couple met again and were to marry when Lori was critically injured. Superman brought a merman from another planet, Ronal, to cure her, but Ronal and Lori fell in love and married. Since that time, Lori has been a close friend of Kal-El.

Lori died during the Crisis defending Tritonis from the Anti-Monitor's shadow creatures.

PSYCHOLOGY & ROLE-PLAYING

Lori is a well-travelled Tritonian, with much experience in the surface world. Even after she was no longer romantically interested in Kal-El, she still had strong feelings for him. She has tried to help him with his romantic entanglements with Lois Lane on several occasions, because she wishes him to have the happiness she has found with Ronal.

NIGHTWING *alias Van-Zee*

DEX:	7	STR:	2	BODY:	6
INT:	7	WILL:	4	MIND:	15
INFL:	3	AURA:	2	SPIRIT:	3
INITIATIVE:	17 (24)	HERO POINTS:	60		

SKILLS: (* linked)
Acrobatics*: 7, Charisma*: 3, Detective*: 7, Gadgetry*: 7, Martial Artist*: 7, Scholar/Training*: 7, Vehicles*: 7, Scientist*: 7

MOTIVATION: Upholding the Good
WEALTH: Affluent
JOB: Scientist
RACE: Normal Humanoid

EQUIPMENT:

FLIGHT BELT

DEX:	0	STR:	3	BODY:	5
CHARGES:	15				
COST:	125 HPs + $ 3400				

POWERS:
Flight: 9

NIGHTMOBILE

DEX:	0	STR:	6	BODY:	8
INT:	0	WILL:	0	MIND:	0
CHARGES:	24				
COST:	330 HPs + $ 165K				

POWERS:
Running: 7, Mind Blank: 12

UTILITY BELT with:

4 Smoke Capsules

DEX:	0	STR:	0	BODY:	1
CHARGES:	12				
COST:	52 HPs + $ 800				

POWERS:
Fog: 7

Laser Torch

DEX:	0	STR:	0	BODY:	1
CHARGES:	1				
COST:	57 HPs + $ 800				

POWERS:
Heat Vision: 7

2 Omni-Gadgets

CLASS A:	1
CLASS C:	3
CLASS D:	4
CHARGES:	10
COST:	* HPs + $ 400

FLAMEBIRD *alias Ak-Var*

DEX:	6	STR:	3	BODY:	7
INT:	5	WILL:	4	MIND:	4
INFL:	3	AURA:	2	SPIRIT:	3
INITIATIVE:	14 (20)	HERO POINTS:	55		

SKILLS: (* linked)
Acrobatics*: 6, Charisma*: 3, Detective*: 5, Gadgetry*: 5, Martial Artist*: 6, Scholar/Training*: 5, Thief*: 6, Vehicles*: 6, Scientist*: 5

MOTIVATION: Upholding the Good
WEALTH: Affluent
JOB: Scientist
RACE: Normal Humanoid
EQUIPMENT:
(Same as Nightwing's)

NIGHTHOUND *(Telepathic Hound)*		
DEX: 3	STR: 3	BODY: 5
INT: 1	WILL: 1	MIND: 3
INFL: 1	AURA: 0	SPIRIT: 1
INITIATIVE: 5	HERO POINTS: 12	

POWERS:
Life Sense: 12

Nightwing and Flamebird are the heroes of Kandor. Originally secret IDs used by a non-powered Superman and Jimmy Olsen, the guises have been taken on by two Kandorian scientists: Van-Zee and Ak-Var.

BACKGROUND

Kandor was once one of the chief cities of the planet Krypton. However, before Jor-El could finish constructing a space ark that would take Kandor's people to safety when Krypton exploded, Brainiac stole the city. The Coluan android used his shrink-ray to reduce Kandor's size, then placed it in a bottle for study. Thus, Kandor became known as the "bottle city."

When some citizens of the bottle city of Kandor enlarged themselves and stole certain elements, Superman and Jimmy Olsen entered Kandor by using a shrinking-ray so that they could investigate. They found out that they were in danger; some Kandorians believed that Superman had a way of enlarging the city and had withheld the information from them. Superman and Jimmy were forced to work "undercover." Inspired by Batman and Robin, the pair modelled their outfits from two Kryptonian birds, the nightwing and the flamebird.

When Superman, trying to pass as his look-alike, Van-Zee, was captured, Van-Zee dressed as Nightwing to rescue him.

In a later adventure, Superman and Jimmy teamed with Batman and Robin (Dick Grayson) in Kandor to battle three metal-skinned villains. They emerged triumphant, and it was during this adventure that Dick Grayson got the idea for his future identity as Nightwing.

Later, a young thief named Ak-Var was released from the Phantom Zone at the end of his sentence and placed in Van-Zee's care, where he was trained as a scientist. Eventually he married Thara, Van-Zee's niece. The two scientists decided that Kandor needed full-time heroes and took on the identities of Nightwing and Flamebird, fighting the occasional Kandorian criminal. On one occasion, Superman and Jimmy Olsen returned to Kandor and the two Nightwing/Flamebird teams joined up.

With Kandor enlarged in recent years, it is not known whether they have been active.

PSYCHOLOGY & ROLE-PLAYING

Although neither Van-Zee or Ak-Var are experienced heroes, their scientific expertise and keen wits have helped them to battle evil, especially since most of the crimes in Kandor are technically-oriented.

Van-Zee, the elder of the two, is a little more introspective and analytical, while Ak-Var tends to leap into things fist-first. Ak-Var views Van-Zee as the father he never really had, and tends to idolize the elder scientist.

VARTOX		
DEX: 22	STR: 45	BODY: 37
INT: 13	WILL: 7	MIND: 13
INFL: 12	AURA: 14	SPIRIT: 15
INITIATIVE: 47	HERO POINTS: 130	

POWERS:
Active Sonar: 15, Animate Image: 20, Broadcast Empath: 25, Comprehend Languages: 13, Earth Animation: 20, Flight: 45, Force Manipulation: 30, Heat Vision: 12, Hypnotism: 25, Illusions: 15, Life Sense: 15, Microscopic Vision: 15, Mind Blast: 20, Object Awareness: 15, Postcognition: 17, Precognition: 17, Recall: 10, Sealed Systems: 20, Skin Armor: 15, Starbolt: 36, Super Breath: 20, Super Hearing: 12, Super Ventriloquism: 15, Systemic Antidote: 20, Telekinesis: 28, Telescopic Vision: 10

SKILLS:
Artist/Actor: 5, Charisma: 7, Detective: 7, Scholar: 6 (Customs of civilizations in Sombrero Hat Galaxy)

LIMITATIONS:
Vartox may only use a total of 75 APs of Powers and Action Attributes per phase. This does not include pushing or spending of Hero Points.

MOTIVATION: Responsibility of Power
WEALTH: NA
JOB: NA
RACE: Normal Humanoid
EQUIPMENT:

LEG JETS		
DEX: 0	STR: 4	BODY: 5
CHARGES: 15		
COST: 85 HPs + $ 700		

POWERS
Flight: 5

TIME SCANSCOPE		
DEX: 0	STR: 0	BODY: 8
INT: 0	WILL: 0	MIND: 0
CHARGES: EPS		
COST: 1280 HPs + $ 3.8B		

POWERS:
Telescopic Vision: 30

A frequent visitor from another galaxy, Vartox has proven himself to be a good friend and a worthy opponent to Superman.

BACKGROUND

Vartox began his career as the champion of Valeron, an Earth-like planet in the Sombrero Hat Galaxy 7-½ million light years (77 APs) away. In addition to Valeron's advanced technology, Vartox has an array of psychic powers of unknown origin.

Vartox's life has been difficult. His first love, Syreena, was a scheming criminal. Later, he married the beautiful Elyra. She died under tragic circumstances which brought him into conflict with Superman.

Vartox once became infected with an agent which caused oxygen atoms to break up. Since Valeron's atmosphere was 90% oxygen, the planet exploded in a chain reaction. When Vartox sought help on Earth, Superman was on hand to keep him from destroying this planet as well.

Moving to Earth for a short period of time, Vartox became romantically involved with Lana Lang. He eventually found a new world to defend, however, and Lana remained on Earth. Vartox now wanders all about his home galaxy, helping to defend against menaces and protect life whenever he is able.

Vartox's self-sacrificing courage and nobility have made him the champion of the Sombrero galaxy. But, he has endured many emotional crises and, in many of these situations, Vartox has borne great guilt. Each emergency has taken its toll; although Vartox is a noble hero, he treads dangerously close to madness at times, becoming a dangerous foe.

When Vartox loses his all-too-precipitous mental balance, he is not likely to become a raving maniac. Instead, he readjusts his view of reality to one in which he bears less guilt. He will subconsciously use his Powers to back up his delusions. Confronting Vartox with reality is sometimes enough to snap him back, although this course of action is dangerous if it fails. When angered, Vartox freely spends Hero Points.

Superman is aware of Vartox's mental instability. Frequently, he will be reluctant to believe Vartox's version of events. Although this may lead to a violent confrontation, they always resolve their differences before parting ways.

ROLE-PLAYING

Superman is Vartox's closest friend. He will come to Superman if he has a problem too big to handle himself. So far, none of Superman's foes has attempted to use Vartox's instabilities against the Man of Tomorrow, but that is not to say that none will.

SUPERWOMAN alias Kristin Wells					
DEX:	6	STR:	2	BODY:	5
INT:	7	WILL:	5	MIND:	5
INFL:	4	AURA:	3	SPIRIT:	3
INITIATIVE:	17		HERO POINTS:		85

SKILLS:
Acrobatics/Dodging: 4, Scholar: 11 (American History — 1763-2100)

LIMITATIONS:
Superwoman must fly in a circle to define the edges of any warps she creates.

MOTIVATION: Responsibility of Power
WEALTH: Affluent
JOB:
29th Century Historian; 20th Century heroine
RACE: Human

EQUIPMENT:

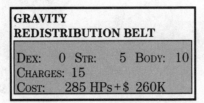

GRAVITY REDISTRIBUTION BELT					
DEX:	0	STR:	5	BODY:	10
CHARGES:	15				
COST:	285 HPs + $ 260K				

POWERS:
Flight: 11

OPAL AMULET					
DEX:	0	STR:	0	BODY:	8
INT:	1	WILL:	0	MIND:	0
CHARGES:	24				
COST:	2349 HPs + $ 9.1B				

POWERS:
Dispersal: 13, Force Field: 30, Gravity Decrease: 14, Recall: 25

TIME-FIELD PROJECTOR WRISTBAND					
DEX:	0	STR:	0	BODY:	7
INT:	0	WILL:	0	MIND:	0
CHARGES:	22				
COST:	1009 HPs + $ 530M				

POWERS:
Gravity Increase: 14, Precognition: 7, Warp: 25

A historian of the year 2862, Kristin Wells travelled back to the 20th Century to research the mysterious heroine known as Superwoman, only to have to take the role herself, thus fulfilling her own destiny.

BACKGROUND

Kristin was a teacher at Columbia University when she was intrigued by the historical records of Superwoman, a heroine of the 20th Century whose identity was unknown even in her time. Kristin travelled back in time and met Superman, whom she had encountered on a previous research mission. By an odd quirk of fate, she found it necessary to take on the role of Superwoman, using 29th-Century technology for her powers.

Kristin assisted Superman in defeating a time-travelling conqueror and returned to her time. When her role as Superwoman became known in her time, she was made a celebrity.

Returning to the 20th Century a year later, her time travel trip was interrupted by a "time storm" which separated Kristin from her memories of her own time.

Still in shock, she wandered around 20th-Century Metropolis. She eventually assisted Superman in thwarting one of Lex Luthor's schemes.

Kristin remained in the 20th Century to play the role of Superwoman for many years. Her exploits after 1986 have yet to be revealed, although it is known that, after eventually regaining her full memory, she returns to the 29th Century.

PSYCHOLOGY

Although Kristin presents a rather flighty appearance to the world, she is a determined woman when faced with a challenge. She views the heroic life as somewhat of a thrill, yet she has a strong responsibility to fill the role of Superwoman. History demands that she play a part, and she has never faltered in her burden.

ROLE-PLAYING

Although Kristin prefers to rely on the technology of the 29th Century to help her to perform her heroics, she is not adverse to closing with an opponent. She is well-trained with her gadgets, having studied them thoroughly before she became aware of her destiny to use them in the role of Superwoman.

As Superman has found on the occasions when he has worked with Kristin, she is mildly irritating due to her historian's knowledge of the 20th Century and her reluctance to share that information for fear of causing possible historical anomalies. She has been known to give history little "pushes" by saying Superman should do something at a certain time, making her seem like what Superman has described as a "space canary."

Kristin's knowledge of the 20th Century is purely historical, with little knowledge of cultural mores, slang, etc. In her first appearances she would speak in wildly inappropriate idioms, but she soon became acclimated to her adopted time.

LEX LUTHOR

DEX:	4	STR:	3	BODY:	4
INT:	14	WILL:	5	MIND:	12
INFL:	8	AURA:	5	SPIRIT:	5
INITIATIVE:	26		HERO POINTS:		160

SKILLS:

Gadgetry: 20, Military
Science/ECM: 12, Scholar: 10
(Astronomy, Computer Science,
History, Mathematics, Psychology,
Biology, Botany, Chemistry,
Electronics, Geology, Robotics),
Scientist: 25, Spy: 13, Vehicles: 11,
Weaponry/ Firearms, Exotic
Weapons, Heavy Weapons: 11

LIMITATIONS:
● Catastrophic Irrational Attraction
for revenge against Superman.
● Catastrophic Miscellaneous on
Teleportation Implant.

MOTIVATION:
Power Lust/Psychopathic
WEALTH: Billionaire
JOB: Criminal Scientist
RACE: Human
EQUIPMENT:

LEXOR BATTLE SUIT

DEX:	22	STR:	26	BODY:	26
CHARGES:	75				
COST:	2742 HPs+ $ 1.54B				

POWERS:
Stretching*: 3

* **Restriction:** only applies to glove
portion of Battle Suit.

POST-LEXOR BATTLE SUIT

DEX:	20	STR:	40	BODY:	37
INT:	3	WILL:	2	MIND:	2
CHARGES:	75				
COST:	13,447 HPs+ $ 43.2T				

POWERS:(* linked)
Bio-Blast*: 37, Flight*: 20, Hypnotism: 12, Illusion: 6, Sealed Systems: 20, Telekinesis: 10

4 OMNI-GADGETS

CLASS A:	3
CLASS B:	3
CLASS C:	20
COST:	* HPs+ $ 26M

Lex Luthor is driven by a psychotic
hatred of Superman. He is, beyond a
doubt, the Man of Steel's most indom-
itable opponent.

BACKGROUND

Ironically, the teenage Lex Luthor
and Superboy first met as friends in
Smallville when Lex saved the Boy of
Steel from Kryptonite exposure. Each
was impressed by the other's great
genius and they became friends.
Superboy built a lab for Luthor in
gratitude.

Luthor devised a cure for Kryptonite poisoning by combining Green
Kryptonite powder with a sample of
artificial protoplasm he had created.
However, in his excitement, Luthor
caused a chemical mishap which
started a fire. Superboy, arriving on
the scene, put out the fire, but the
chemical fumes caused Luthor's hair
to fall out. Apparently, the fumes also
affected his mind.

The protoplasm was irretrievably
lost in the fire. Luthor, enraged,
blamed everything on Superboy. He
attempted to gain fame with other
inventions; with each failure he grew

more incensed, blaming his bad luck on Superboy's intervention. Luthor turned to crime. His horrified parents disowned him, took the name of Thorul, and moved away. They told their daughter Lena that Lex had died in a mountain-climbing accident.

Lex spent years in and out of reformatories, constantly bedeviling Superboy. He earned a solid reputation in the criminal underworld as a genius second to none, and he acquired millions of dollars with patents filed under false names.

When Kal-El began his career as Superman in Metropolis, Lex was on hand as the first of many villains to challenge the Man of Tomorrow. Although his primary goal was the destruction of Superman, his hatred of society grew to the point where he sought total control of Metropolis, America and, eventually, the world.

On one occasion, Luthor lured Superman to a duel on a world orbiting a red sun. They discovered a declining civilization there which was desperately in need of water. During their battle, Luthor tried to help the natives. Unable to bring them the liquid they needed, Luthor forfeited the duel in return for Superman's promise to deliver the water. But the natives were unaware of the arrangement. They revered Luthor as a hero, naming the planet Lexor in his honor.

On a later trip to Lexor he married a young woman, Ardora, who bore Lex a son, Lex, Jr. During this stay, Lex used his scientific knowledge to bring the civilization back from the brink of savagery. Although he now lived on Lexor as a hero, he nonetheless returned to Earth again and again to continue his feud with Superman. Each scheme was more intricate and diabolical than the last.

During one stay on Lexor, Luthor discovered a suit of ancient battle-armor. Mastering its secrets, Lex lured Superman to Lexor once more hoping to destroy him with the new weaponry. However, his plan backfired and Luthor's second home was obliterated. Naturally, Lex blamed the destruction on Superman.

After transporting a piece of Lexor to the Atlantic to form an island for his new headquarters, Lex launched one of his most nefarious schemes yet: a mental assault on Superman to convince him of the destruction of Earth. Luthor, not knowing about Superman's double identity, believed Superman and Clark Kent to be close friends. Lex thought that Superman would not only suffer mental anguish over the Earth's "destruction," but that the Man of Steel would suffer twofold when he inadvertently ruined his friend's professional reputation by giving him false information for a news story. However, Lex's best-laid plans failed once more, and Superman tracked Luthor to his new lair and captured him.

When Luthor was last seen, he had escaped again, but he was forced to enlist Superman's help to prevent his death at the hands of his own battle suit, which was possessed by a sinister electronic intelligence. The intelligence was destroyed and Luthor recaptured, but the suit made a preprogrammed escape and presumably still waits to rescue its master at an opportune moment.

PSYCHOLOGY

Lex Luthor is a driven man: driven by his hatred of Superman, driven by the rejection he believes he suffered as a youth, and driven by his incredible ambition to be nothing less than the "greatest" man in the world.

Luthor holds everyone in disdain, and often strokes his own ego by surrounding himself with dimwitted henchmen. For all this, Lex is a bundle of contradictions. He eventually discovered the location of his sister Lena and, before she became aware of the fact that he was alive, he went to great pains to insure that she learned nothing of his criminal activities. Despite his loathing for Superman and other heroes, he sought the adulation of the people of Lexor. If Luthor is properly approached, he can be convinced to contribute his genius to projects of great good. Sometimes he may take up such a project to prove to the world he can do something that Superman can't.

METHODS

Foremost in Luthor's vast arsenal is his incredible intellect. It is fortunate that he has selected one of the most resourceful men alive as the target of his hatred: it is unlikely that anyone but Superman could withstand Luthor's years of investigation, study, and contemplation.

Lex's schemes against Superman are quite complex. However, he is slow to learn from his mistakes; with many of his early plans, he did not take Superman's extraordinary abilities into account. In the last few years, Lex has relied more on mental assaults and psychological warfare.

Although Lex often derides Superman as a "muscle-bound oaf," he seems to obtain great satisfaction from surpassing Superman on a physical level when he modifies the odds in his favor. His current battle-suit makes him Superman's near-equal in strength. However, after years of defeat, Luthor intends for Superman to suffer in ways no mere physical beating could do.

ROLE-PLAYING

Lex Luthor's foremost goal is the destruction of Superman. In his mind, nothing else counts. He is convinced that only pure luck has allowed the strong buffoon to survive so many attacks that he himself, the Earth's greatest criminal, master-minded.

Luthor considers himself the mental superior of everyone on Earth. He has a grudging respect for Brainiac's computer intellect, but argues the Coluan android is ultimately inferior because the android lacks emotions.

Lex has allied himself with Brainiac on a number of occasions, but his ego allows him no "partners." Luthor's inability to work with others is illustrated by his dealings with the Secret Society of Super-Villains. Stalking into their headquarters, Luthor declared himself their leader, recruited three magicians to defeat Superman, then blamed the Secret Society of Super-Villains when his plan failed.

Lex Luthor's plots are rarely "short and sweet," and any Gamemaster employing the criminal genius as an opponent should develop a series of minor battles leading up to a climactic showdown with Luthor himself.

BRAINIAC *Original Coluan/Humanoid Form*

DEX:	12	STR:	9	BODY:	22
INT:	26	WILL:	15	MIND:	23
INFL:	2	AURA:	3	SPIRIT:	2
INITIATIVE:	40	HERO POINTS:	150		
CHARGES:	NA				
COST:	10025 HPs + $ 3.01T				

POWERS:

Force Field: 40, Recall: 30, Regeneration: 9, Sealed Systems: 20

SKILLS:

Charisma/Intimidation: 8, Gadgetry: 16, Medicine: 12, Military Science/Cartography, ECM: 12, Scholar: 12 (all known fields of science), Scientist: 30, Vehicles/Space: 22

RACE: Artificial Life (android)

EQUIPMENT:

SPACESHIP

DEX:	0	STR:	18	BODY:	25
INT:	5	WILL:	0	MIND:	0
CHARGES:	20				
COST:	13465 HPs + $ 12T				

POWERS:

Flight: 24, Force Field: 40, Radar Sense: 25, Sealed Systems: 28, Super Ventriloquism: 30, Warp: 45 (speed)

BRAINIAC *Dispersed Form*

DEX:	8	STR:	15	BODY:	6
INT:	26	WILL:	20	MIND:	30
INFL:	3	AURA:	4	SPIRIT:	4
INITIATIVE:	37(53)	HERO POINTS:	195		

POWERS:

Dispersal: 30, Recall: 40, Sealed Systems: 25

SKILLS:

Charisma/Intimidation: 14, Gadgetry: 20, Martial Artist: 16, Medicine: 20, Military Science/Cartography & ECM: 20, Scholar: 20 (all known fields of science), Scientist: 35, Vehicles/Space: 45

LIMITATIONS:

Dispersal is permanently on: Brainiac must occupy machine body to make Physical attacks and gain manipulatory appendages.

MOTIVATION: Power Lust

WEALTH: NA

JOB: NA

RACE: Artificial Life

EQUIPMENT:

MACHINE BODY

DEX:	0	STR:	15	BODY:	39
CHARGES:	49				
COST:	2170 HPs + $ 3Q				

POWERS:

Lightning: 15

SPACESHIP

DEX:	0	STR:	25	BODY:	50
INT:	8	WILL:	0	MIND:	0
CHARGES:	23				
COST:	22,350 HPs + $ 126.5T				

POWERS:

Flight: 23, Radar Sense: 28, Sealed Systems: 30, Super Ventriloquism: 44, Warp: 45 (Speed)

Brainiac is the ultimate evolution of mechanical sentience; he is a unique form of organic life. He pursues his goal of destroying Superman with single-minded ruthlessness.

BACKGROUND

Brainiac was first created by the computers of the planet Colu. Determined to overthrow their organic masters, they crafted Brainiac as a spy, complete with the duplicated mental patterns of a Coluan scientist. To complete the disguise, Brainiac was given a "son," who was forced to pose as his kin.

After the computers took over Colu, Brainiac was sent into space armed with a powerful shrinking ray. His mission: to steal samples from other worlds to be tested for possible conquest. These were actually whole cities miniaturized for easy transportation. One of the first shrunken cities collected by Brainiac was Kandor from the planet Krypton. It was this theft that destroyed the hopes of Jor-El, Krypton's leading scientist, and led him to decide to use rocket ships to evacuate his people.

While Brainiac was away, his adopted "son", Vril Dox, determined a means of elevating his intelligence to the 12th logarithmic level, giving himself a "computer mind." So aided, Vril led the Coluans in a revolt against their mechanical usurpers. The rebellion was successful, and the secret of acquiring 12th-level intelligence was passed along to Vril's descendants. One of these descendants, Querl Dox (Brainiac 5), is a member of the 30th-Century Legion of Super-Heroes.

Brainiac first encountered Superman some years later while attempting to steal Metropolis. Unable to penetrate Brainiac's force field, Superman allowed himself to be captured with Metropolis. After Brainiac entered suspended animation, Superman returned Metropolis and the other stolen cities and took Kandor to his Fortress of Solitude.

When Brainiac returned to Colu and found his masters defeated, he set out to conquer the universe. He frequently returned to Earth to seek vengeance against Superman.

After one defeat, Brainiac was left entombed in a mechanical world of his own creation. With no other means of escape, the android forced the system's sun to go nova, but miscalculated the energies involved and was reduced to a dispersed cloud of molecules.

In this dispersed state, Brainiac drifted through space. He encountered a planet of living machines from which he absorbed the equivalent of millions of years of knowledge. This process totally stripped away his human mannerisms. He drifted about the universe, gathering more data.

Brainiac finally returned to the computerized world and used its machinery to reintegrate himself to a state in which he could do more than simply gather knowledge. He created metallic bodies of a "living metal" to give his formless mass of energy arms and legs, and designed a vast spaceship of the same material.

During his "death," Brainiac had thought he glimpsed a giant hand belonging to an entity called "the Master Programmer." Confused memories of his numerous defeats led him to believe that Superman was the Programmer's "Angel of Death." Brainiac is now convinced that the only way he can achieve his ultimate goal of universal conquest is to destroy the Master Programmer and Angel of Death. He plans to do this no matter what the cost.

PSYCHOLOGY

In his Coluan android form, Brainiac possessed some of the mannerisms of a human being, but had no real understanding of human psychology. The only emotion that he possessed was the desire for power, which was programmed into him by his computer creators.

As an android with a 12th-level intellect, Brainiac usually considered himself above physical conflict, relying on his near-impenetrable force field for protection from any dangers.

Ironically, Brainiac's "death" in the nova caused his birth as an electrical form of intelligence, but an intelligence possessing completely negative qualities: a lust for power, fear, hate, contempt, and a lack of compassion. Brainiac's goal of conquest is now no longer merely a programmed objective, but a goal that he seeks for his own self-aggrandizement.

As a "computerized" intelligence, Brainiac seeks order. He views the universe as teeming with billions and billions of chaotic organisms. He is driven by two things: the desire to make order by eradicating chaos, and fear of his own destruction by the Master Programmer.

METHODS

As a coldly logical intelligence with no compassion or any other emotional "weaknesses," Brainiac will do whatever he has to in order to obtain his goals. If destroying the solar system would result in Superman's destruction, then he would do so without flinching a transistor, no matter the cost in human life.

Aboard his ship Brainiac maintains several platoons of well-armed troops. These soldiers are the survivors of worlds that Brainiac has already destroyed; the soldiers serve him because their only other choice is death. They bear no loyalty to their master, and Brainiac does not hesitate to use them as cannon fodder. On the contrary, Brainiac finds his equivalent of satisfaction in redirecting units of chaos to wipe out other forces of chaos.

The Gamemaster should keep in mind that Brainiac will do whatever is necessary to obtain his goals. While Luthor would (and often has) hesi-

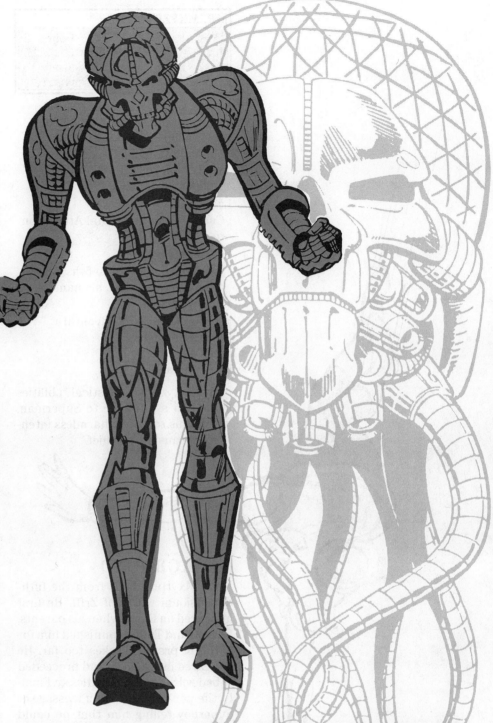

tate to wipe out Earth, Brainiac would show no mercy.

ROLE-PLAYING

Brainiac is now an organic life form, but he still retains much of his previous android "personality." The only human characteristic he displays when dealing with others is arrogance. He knows that he is superior to other life forms.

Before his transformation, Brainiac often allied with Superman's other archfoe, Lex Luthor. He considered

Luthor's intelligence and insights valuable in the fight against the Man of Tomorrow. However, on a number of occasions, Brainiac did not hesitate to double-cross Luthor once Luthor had become a non-essential.

The "new" Brainiac is almost entirely self-sufficient. His new capabilities allow him to conquer most planets with relative ease. He chose to ally with Lex Luthor during the Crisis, however, and would certainly do so again in the interests of self-preservation. Such alliances would be fraught with intrigue.

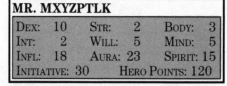

POWERS:

Animate Image: 20, Flight: 10, Invisibility: 15, Matter Manipulation: 25, Super Ventriloquism: 10, Teleportation: 20

LIMITATIONS:

Catastrophic Irrational Attraction to practical jokes

VULNERABILITIES:

Will be transported to 5th dimension if he says his name backwards.

MOTIVATION: Thrill of Adventure
WEALTH: Struggling
JOB: NA
RACE: Humanoid

Mr. Mxyzptlk's Mystical abilities make him a nuisance to Superman, despite his relatively harmless intentions of causing mischief.

BACKGROUND

Mr. Mxyzptlk hails from the fifth-dimensional world of Zrfff. He first appeared on Earth when his parents, Fuzastl and Tindsa, punished him for carrying practical jokes too far. He appeared in Smallvile and proceeded to bedevil Superboy relentlessly. Finally, the imp's father sent a message to Superboy telling him that he could banish Mxyzptlk from Earth for at least 90 days by tricking him into speaking or spelling his name backwards. Superboy immediately made use of this advice, but Mxyzptlk returned to plague him as an adult. Over the years Mxyzptlk has returned again and again, each time with some new way to embarrass Superman.

Recently, Mxyzptlk married Mrs. Bgbyny, an incredibly homely Zrfffian imp who tricked him into marrying her by using magic to beautify herself. The marriage was annulled when she revealed her true appearance, but not before Mxyzptlk had a son, Kytszbtn. It is known that Mxyzptlk has at least one descendent who has lived to the 30th Century. Taking the name of his 20th-Century ancestor, this Mxyzptlk has teamed with the 30th Century descendant of Lex Luthor and joined the adult Legion of Super Heroes.

METHODS

The only limit to Mxyzptlk's Mystical Powers is his vivid imagination. In the past his stunts have included: wiping the memory of Superman from every citizen of Metropolis, running a newspaper in competition to the Daily Planet with "future news," becoming "Super-Mxyzptlk" to gain public adulation, making Superman's Powers uncontrollably transferable, turning the U.S. into a giant chessboard, and reversing the sexes of everyone in Metropolis.

Mxyzptlk's only real weakness is his infinite gullibility in being tricked into speaking his name backwards. He has tried a number of tricks to avoid this, including remaining underwater, taking out a fifth-dimensional "insurance policy," putting an alarm in his hat, etc. Superman has always managed to outwit the imp, however.

ROLE-PLAYING

Mr. Mxyzptlk comes from a race of egocentrics; he is the worst of the lot. His main goal in life is to make Superman's life miserable, but, like the Joker's involvement with Batman, he has no desire to lose his sparring partner. On several occasions, when more vicious villains have used his magic to try to kill Superman, he has willingly returned to Zrfff and caused all of his magic to dissipate rather than see Superman die.

Another of Mxyzptlk's major flaws is his vanity. He considers himself a "handsome heroic figure . . . greater even than Superman . . .". Lois Lane and others have overwhelmed him with flattery, then tricked him into reciting his name backwards. On another occasion, Superman convinced Mxyzptlk that the world was laughing at him so that he would voluntarily return to Zrfff rather than face further humiliation.

BIZARRO

DEX:	26	STR:	50	BODY:	40
INT:	13	WILL:	12	MIND:	17
INFL:	4	AURA:	3	SPIRIT:	5
INITIATIVE:	43		HERO POINTS:	75	

CHARGES: 61
COST: 28,848 HPs + $ 225QN

POWERS:

Directional Hearing: 10, Extended Hearing: 10, Flame Projection: 15, Flight: 45, Force Manipulation (eyes): 15, Ice Production (eyes): 30, Invulnerability: 50, Sealed Systems: 20, Super Hearing: 10, Superspeed: 25, Systemic Antidote: 20, Telekinesis: 15, Thermal Vision: 15, X-Ray Vision: 20

SKILLS:

Charisma/Persuasion: 7

LIMITATIONS:

●Bizarro thinks in reverse in many ways.

●Force Manipulation can only be used to shrink objects.

●Telekinesis can only be used to move objects directly away.

●X-Ray Vision can only see through lead.

VULNERABILITIES:

Rare Fatal Vulnerability
Blue Kryptonite: Range: 3

MOTIVATION: NA

WEALTH: NA

JOB: Ruler of Bizarro World

RACE: Artificial Life (true android)

EQUIPMENT:

SUPER UNIFORM

DEX:	0	STR:	0	BODY:	25
CHARGES:	NA				
COST:	991 HPs + $ 350M				

POWERS:
Skin Armor: 10

Like Mr. Mxyzptlk, Bizarro bears no actual malice towards Superman, but his bizarre reverse mode of logic inevitably leads him into conflict with Superman, the only one capable of handling the devastation that results when Bizarro comes visiting.

BACKGROUND

Bizarro is an artificial life form created by Lex Luthor. Luthor reconstructed a Duplicator Ray machine from the plans of a Professor Delton who used the machine on Superboy years before. Although Luthor was not sure what would result, he exposed Superman to the machine's rays. What resulted was a bizarre construction of lifeless matter, in the form of Superman, possessed of a strange form of reversed sentience. Dubbing the weird creature "Bizarro," Luthor tried to command his creation, only to discover Bizarro possessed a life of his own.

Sickened at his ugly countenance in a mirror, Bizarro captured Luthor and deposited his prisoner at the nearby police station, only to be rebuffed by a public frightened by his inhuman stone-like face. The pathetic creature then fell in love with Lois Lane, who was able to distract his amorous attentions by creating a duplicate of herself with Luthor's machine. Taking Luthor's duplication machine with them, Bizarro and Bizarro-Lois left Earth to find a home for themselves.

The couple eventually found a suitable, deserted world, which they populated with duplicates of themselves. On his first visit, Superman reshaped the newly rechristened planet "Htrae" into a cube. Since then, Bizarro has visited Earth several times to visit "Me good enemy, Superman." Fortunately, the rest of the Bizarros are mostly stay-at-homes and Superman has rarely had trouble with them.

METHODS

Bizarro really has no methods; he tends to rely on brute force to settle anything which he perceives as a problem. Sophisticated strategies are totally beyond him.

Bizarro's logic has always been reversed; a collision with a meteor of unknown origins reversed several of Bizarro's Powers as well, giving him Ice Vision instead of Heat Vision, Flame Breath instead of Ice Breath, Telescopic Vision which, instead of making faraway objects seem close, actually makes nearby objects move further away, Microscopic Vision which, instead of making small objects seem large, actually makes large objects grow smaller, and X-Ray Vision which sees through nothing but lead.

ROLE-PLAYING

Despite his warped thinking, Bizarro means well, but his logic works in reverse from "normal" logic: he sees good as bad, bad as good, friends as enemies, and enemies as friends. Since he thinks of Superman as a "friend," he attacks him, declaring his "friendship" all the while. On his homeworld, the Bizarros enjoy eating cold dogs, work on Saturdays and Sundays, and watch film negatives.

Bizarro should be treated primarily as a nuisance, and never as a deliberate antagonist.

MONGUL

DEX:	23	STR:	52	BODY:	60
INT:	15	WILL:	20	MIND:	25
INFL:	12	AURA:	10	SPIRIT:	30
INITIATIVE:	50		HERO POINTS:	165	

POWERS:

Sealed Systems: 20, Starbolt: 38

SKILLS:

Charisma/Interrogation, Intimidation: 15, Gadgetry: 17, Military Science/ECM: 12, Spy/Coding: 8, Vehicles: 14

EQUIPMENT:

CONTAINMENT CUBES

DEX:	0	STR:	2	BODY:	10
INT:	0	WILL:	0	MIND:	0
CHARGES:	53				
COST:	4466 HPs + $ 3.25T				

POWERS:

Force Manipulation (Shrinking only): 8, Neutralize: 45

SPACESHIP

DEX:	0	STR:	20	BODY:	40
INT:	5	WILL:	0	MIND:	0
CHARGES:	IPS				
COST:	14,030 HPs + $ 10.95T				

POWERS:

Flight: 23, Matter Manipulation: 20, Radar Sense: 28, Sealed Systems: 28, Super Ventriloquism: 30

TELEPORTATION BELT

DEX:	0	STR:	0	BODY:	15
INT:	0	WILL:	0	MIND:	0
CHARGES:	70				
COST:	725 HPs + $ 35M				

POWERS:

Teleportation: 20

MOTIVATION: Power Lust
WEALTH: NA
JOB: Conqueror
RACE: Strange Humanoid

Mongul is one of Superman's most formidable foes, despite his relatively recent addition to the Man of Tomorrow's Rogues Gallery. He is more than a match, both physically and mentally, for Superman.

BACKGROUND

Little is known of Mongul's history prior to his first meeting with Superman. Mongul claimed to have been the absolute ruler of his home planet, but his subjects eventually rose up and overthrew him. He fled and, sometime later, gained special Physical Powers that put him on a par with Superman. Setting his sights on galactic rule, Mongul held Lois Lane, Steve Lombard, and Jimmy Olsen hostage to force Superman to contend with J'onn J'onzz for a crystal key. The key gave Mongul cybernetic control of an alien Warworld. But, when Mongul was forced to use the Warworld against Superman and Supergirl, his brain cortex was severely overloaded and he almost met the fate that the Warworld's creators had suffered.

Automatic teleport devices prevented Mongul's capture. After Mongul recovered, he attempted to gain control of an alien Empire ruled by the otherwordly Starman. With Superman's assistance, Mongul was thwarted once more. Mongul later attempted to destroy Earth by gaining control of a Sun-Eater from a 20th Century Controller. He set it on a course for Earth, but he was captured and the Sun-Eater was destroyed, thanks to the intervention of the Legion of Super-Heroes.

Mongul later escaped captivity and, striking at Superman directly, ensnared him in a "black mercy," a semi-intelligent plant/fungus that feeds off of its victim's bio-aura while supplying him or her with their happiest dreams to keep them immobile. Superman was able to break the hypnotic trance when his dream of growing to manhood on an intact Krypton turned into a nightmare. Mongul himself was caught in the black mercy's grip and is currently in a trance, dreaming of his vast conquest of the universe.

METHODS

Mongul only has two goals: the humiliation and death of Superman, and absolute power over the peoples of the universe. He is a careful planner despite his megalomania. It is usually some factor beyond his control that robs him of victory.

Mongul is a master of technology. His strength is a match for Superman's, and his transporter technology is among the best in the known universe. He has also created special trans-dimensional force fields that shrink and can negate the powers of a specific target.

ROLE-PLAYING

Mongul is one of Superman's most ruthless opponents. His wish for galactic rule makes him even more dangerous, than Superman-haters like Luthor or bandit/robber types like Terra-Man.

Mongul is totally self-reliant. His ego permits him no henchmen or confidants; he has nothing but contempt for individuals of a lesser power level than his own.

Despite this scorn, Mongul will go to the ends of the universe to obtain revenge on anyone who interferes in his plans for galactic domination. Unfortunately, he never becomes foolhardy when pursuing vengeance.

TERRA-MAN alias Toby Manning

DEX:	23	STR:	4	BODY:	8
INT:	8	WILL:	5	MIND:	7
INFL:	5	AURA:	3	SPIRIT:	63
INITIATIVE:	36		HERO POINTS:	160	

POWERS:

Sealed Systems: 20

SKILLS:

Animal Handling: 6, Detective/Law & Police Procedure: 5, Gadgetry/Build Gadget: 14, Medicine/First Aid: 5, Military Science/Camouflage, ECM and Tracking: 6, Scholar/Academic (Western Lore): 9, Weaponry: 20

LIMITATIONS:

Serious Irrational Attraction: The Wild West

CONNECTIONS:

Intergalactic Underworld (high-level)

MOTIVATION: Mercenary
WEALTH: Multimillionaire
JOB: Professional Criminal
RACE: Human

EQUIPMENT:

SIX-SHOOTER

DEX:	0	STR:	0	BODY:	8
CHARGES:	6				
COST:	560 HPs + $ 150M				

POWERS:

Projectile Weapons: 22

BULLETS

DEX:	18	STR:	0	BODY:	5
INT:	2	WILL:	0	MIND:	0
CHARGES:	1				
COST:	1322 HPs + $ 310M				

POWERS:

Bomb: 22, Thermal (IR) Vision: 15

NOTE: Bullets are "heat-seekers," and will follow target as long as they can follow heat trace of original target or until destroyed.

OMNI-GADGET

CLASS A:	8
CLASS B:	7
CLASS C:	7
COST:	* HPs + $ 4400

NOVA *Arguvian Space Steed (Winged Horse)*

DEX:	7	STR:	3	BODY:	7
INT:	1	WILL:	0	MIND:	1
INFL:	1	AURA:	0	SPIRIT:	1
INITIATIVE:	9	HERO POINTS:	0		

POWERS:

Flight: 44, Sealed Systems: 30

Terra-Man is an oddity as a member of Superman's Rogues Gallery. His bizarre background has led him to pick Superman, Earth's "Head Lawman" as his arch-enemy, for he would be comfortable fighting almost any hero. Although his anachronistic mannerisms make him easy to underestimate, he has mastered superscientific technology, dealt with numerous alien races, and fought Superman to a standstill on many occasions.

BACKGROUND

Terra-Man was born Toby Manning, the son of Jess Manning, a notorious outlaw of the 1880's. His father was accidently killed by an alien criminal thrill-seeker known as "The Collector" in a moment of fury. The Collector, to make up for the death of a man who had only wounded him, decided to raise Toby as a criminal, as his father had intended.

Using a hypnotic grid, the Collector wiped the boy's memory of Jess' death and took the boy with him into space. He placed devices in the boy's body that would allow him to survive in

any environment and tutored Toby in the use of advanced technology. Toby altered some high-tech items to resemble objects from his Old West childhood. He captured and broke an Arguvian Space-Steed, a kind of winged horse which he named Nova. Taking the name of his home planet, Toby adopted the guise of "Terra-Man" and began committing crimes for the Collector.

Eventually, Toby deciphered a clue his father had left before dying and avenged his father by killing the Collector. Although he had been in space for nearly a century, relativistic time dilation had slowed his aging so that he was a young man. He returned to Earth to continue his criminal career and contend with the galaxy's Number One lawman.

METHODS

Although he has no natural powers, Terra-Man possesses an unlimited arsenal of hi-tech weapons disguised as western objects. His mentality combines the attitudes of an 1880's Wild West outlaw with those of a 20th-Century villain. As with most of Superman's foes, he is well-schooled in the use of diversionary tactics. Although he likes to meet Superman in a "showdown" whenever possible, such a meeting will always be rigged in his favor. Oddly enough, he never seems to exploit Superman's weaknesses; this outlook is likely to be an equivalent of the "never shoot a man in the back" gunfighters' code.

ROLE-PLAYING

Terra-Man's personality is based on his only two sources of the 1880's Old West: his own glamorized childhood memories and 20th-Century movies and TV shows. He adheres to the media-reported codes of the Wild West: he never shoots a man in the back and never intentionally hurts innocents. He is not a very intricate schemer. Although Terra-Man would be happy to kill Superman, just as an 1880's outlaw wouldn't have hesitated to shoot a famous lawman, he is not obsessed with Superman's death the way many of Superman's foes, such as Luthor and Brainiac, are. He seems to enjoy matching wits with the Man of Tomorrow.

TOYMAN alias Winslow P. Schott

DEX:	5	STR:	2	BODY:	4
INT:	9	WILL:	5	MIND:	6
INFL:	5	AURA:	3	SPIRIT:	4
INITIATIVE:	19	HERO POINTS:	95		

SKILLS:
Charisma: 4, Gadgetry: 12,
Scholar/Academic Study
(Toys): 11, Vehicles: 4, Weaponry: 8

LIMITATIONS:
Catastrophic Irrational Attraction:
Toys

CONNECTIONS:
Most toy companies (low-level)
Metropolis Underworld (low-level)

MOTIVATION: Psychopath
WEALTH: Affluent
JOB: Toymaker, Professional Criminal
RACE: Human

EQUIPMENT:

5 OMNI-GADGETS

CLASS A.:	7
CLASS C.:	7
CLASS D.:	8
CHARGES:	12
COST:	* HPs + $ 4400

Although presenting an eccentric, slightly ludicrous figure to the world, the Toyman is a formidable and persistent foe of Superman's despite his odd appearance.

BACKGROUND

Little is known of Schott's history and youth. It seems that he was driven to crime when a neighborhood bully, Chester Y. Dunholtz, destroyed his first homemade toy.

The Toyman first appeared on the scene as "the world's cleverest toymaker". Despite his fame, Schott felt that people were laughing at him behind his back, and he retaliated with a crime spree. Schott was finally brought to justice moments before Lois Lane was to die at the hands of his poison-nailed mechanical dolls.

Despite numerous failures, the Toyman has always returned for more, trying to get the last laugh on the world he hates. At one point, Winslow decided to retire and go straight. He even teamed up with Superman on one occasion when a young criminal genius named Jack

Nimball took the name of "Toyman" for his criminal doings.

It was during an unfortunate incident when Bizarro wrecked Schott's exhibit at an inventor's exposition that Winslow went berserk. Mistaking the imperfect Superman as the real thing, Winslow returned to crime with a vengeance, killing Nimball. Even after learning the truth about the exposition incident, he continued his criminal career.

Schott seemed to reform once more, and acted as a consultant for several toy companies. He also ran a Toyman Trivia Contest on network TV, but it turned out to be a ploy to lure his childhood nemesis, Chester Dunholtz, into the open. Superman saved the hapless Dunholtz from the Toyman's wrath after Chester was unable to return the destroyed toy from years gone by.

METHODS

Schott utilizes any number of intricate mechanical devices in committing crimes. Many of them are explosives, which he uses for diversions. He employs many vehicle-like toys for quick escapes. The Toyman has also used simple toys, like tops and yoyos, made out of Kryptonite.

Although the Toyman's crimes all involve the use of toys, the crimes themselves are usually for monetary gain. Schott would be more likely to go for an armored car heist than a jewelled toy collection theft, perhaps due to his fear of destroying such valuable toys through mishap.

ROLE-PLAYING

Despite his eccentric and somewhat kindly appearance, the Toyman is a malevolent criminal mastermind, almost on a par with the Joker. He has killed or attempted to kill on numerous occasions. His childhood experiences drive him to overcompensate for his affable appearance by being extremely ruthless.

Schott, like many other Superman villains, is not powerful enough to take on his arch-foe face-to-face, and his toys are rarely powerful enough to harm Superman. As such, he is an intricate schemer and his plans are always diabolical in their ingenuity.

GALACTIC GOLEM

DEX:	20	STR:	52	BODY:	57
INT:	1	WILL:	0	MIND:	0
INFL:	0	AURA:	0	SPIRIT:	0
INITIATIVE:	21	HERO POINTS:	105		
CHARGES:	EPS (10 charge reserve)				
COST:	24,293 HPs + $ 1.94Q				

POWERS:
Running: 4, Sealed Systems: 30,
Systemic Antidote: 30

LIMITATIONS:
Power Limitation: For each 7 APs the Golem goes without a dose of "hyperstellar energy," reduce its STR and BODY by 1 AP to a maximum reduction of 20 APs per Attribute.

MOTIVATION: NA
WEALTH: NA
JOB: Pawn
RACE: Artificial Life (true android)

A creation of Lex Luthor, the Golem is a modern-day equivalent of the Frankenstein monster. It is a nearly unstoppable menace.

BACKGROUND

The Golem was created by Lex Luthor; it was intended as a weapon against Superman. Since the Golem gains its energy from all the stars in the heavens rather than from Earth's yellow sun alone, Luthor assumed that the Golem would emerge triumphant. Superman defeated the Golem and it turned on its creator. Luthor was then forced to send it off Earth to save his own life.

The Golem has appeared several times since, retaining its antagonism towards Superman. There are conflicting reports as to its current whereabouts; it is apparent that the Golem is not gone forever.

METHODS

The Golem's INT of 1 only allows it to gather and collate information so that it can move; it is incapable of any subtle planning. It can home in on the solar energies in Superman's body no matter where on Earth those energies are, and is a relentless pursuer.

ROLE-PLAYING

Although Luthor has abandoned the Golem as a failed experiment, other villains might use it as a powerful pawn. The intervention of another more intelligent villain will be necessary in order for the Golem to recover enough hyper-stellar energy to operate or, according to some reports, return to Earth. In any case, the Golem is a berserker, unable to be reasoned with and impossible to be controlled except under very extraordinary circumstances.

PRANKSTER *alias Oswald Loomis*			
Dex: 4	Str: 2	Body: 4
Int: 7	Will: 3	Mind: 4
Infl: 4	Aura: 3	Spirit: 3
Initiative: 15		Hero Points: 45

Equipment:

2 OMNI-GADGETS	
Class A:	3
Class C:	3
Charges:	10
Cost:	* HPs + $ 120

Skills:
Charisma: 6, Detective/Law: 4, Gadgetry: 5, Vehicles: 3

Limitations:
Serious Irrational Attraction: Practical Jokes

Motivation: Thrillseeker
Wealth: Comfortable
Job: Professional Criminal
Race: Human

The Prankster is one of Superman's lesser known enemies. He has proven himself to be a determined, ruthless foe despite his bizarre appearance.

BACKGROUND

Nothing is known of Loomis prior to his first crimes as the Prankster: mock holdups in which he gave money to banks. These "robberies" were actually a ruse; the last bank robbery was for real.

Since then the Prankster has returned many times. With each new appearance there is some scheme more outlandish than the last. On one occasion he had an inside man at the U.S. Copyright Office so he could copyright the alphabet; another time, in order to lure a millionaire into the open, he set up a statue that would supposedly grant wishes. However, the Prankster has been relatively quiet in recent years, except for a partnership with the Joker which backfired into a brush with death by Joker-venom.

METHODS

The Prankster almost always uses some bizarre kind of swindle to gain money by illegal means: the more outlandish, the better. Although the Prankster will sometimes use practical joke items as weapons, he does not commit "practical joke" theme crimes or anything of that sort.

ROLE-PLAYING

Despite his appearance, Loomis is extremely ruthless. He speaks in high-sounding phrases, saying "Aye, verily!" instead of "Yes," for instance. He is not to be underestimated.

```
LORD SATANIS
DEX:   11    STR:    5    BODY:   16
INT:   15    WILL:  17    MIND:   22
INFL:  15    AURA:  26    SPIRIT: 32
INITIATIVE: 41    HERO POINTS: 175
```

POWERS:

Magical Sense: 21, Magic Blast: 24, Magic Shield: 10, *Mystic Link —* Force Manipulation: 36, Spirit Travel: 18

SKILLS:

Charisma: 11, Occultist: 24, Scholar/Academic Study (Mystic Lore): 24

MOTIVATION: Power Lust
WEALTH: Multimillionaire
JOB: Sorcerer
RACE: Humanoid

```
SYRENE
DEX:    9    STR:    4    BODY:   14
INT:   14    WILL:  15    MIND:   22
INFL:  17    AURA:  29    SPIRIT: 36
INITIATIVE: 40    HERO POINTS: 150
```

POWERS:

Magical Sense: 24, Magic Blast: 27, Magic Shield: 13, *Mystic Link —* Force Manipulation: 39, Spirit Travel: 18

SKILLS:

Charisma: 13, Occultist: 24, Scholar/Academic Study (Mystic Lore): 24

LIMITATIONS:

Power Limitation: Without the Runestone of Merlin (see

Background), reduce all of Syrene's Attributes and Powers higher than Lord Satanis' to the same value as his.

MOTIVATION: Power Lust
WEALTH: Multimillionaire
JOB: Sorceress
RACE: Human

Due to their vast Mystical Powers and their intelligence, Lord Satanis and Syrene are two of Superman's most deadly magical opponents.

BACKGROUND

Little is known of Lord Satanis' background. He took his name from the Lord of Lies; his real name is unknown, and his face has never been revealed. Although he claimed to come from a "dimension-lost world," he rose to power on the magic-oriented world of a million years hence. His main rival was Ambra, ruler of Earth and possessor of the mystic Runestone of Merlin.

Satanis led a revolt of sorcerers against Ambra and his daughter, Syrene, who also sought the throne but was unable to oppose her father as long as he held the runestone. Ambra was defeated and killed, but, with his dying breath, he sent the source of his incredible powers back to a random time in history.

Both Satanis and Syrene wished to take over the throne, but neither possessed the power to defeat the other. Rather than waste their energies, they agreed to a marriage of convenience and ruled the Earth together. However, each secretly sought a spell to travel back through time to recover the runestone.

Satanis and Syrene discovered the correct spell at nearly the same time, and they travelled back to the 20th Century. The key to triggering the powers of the runestone was to filter the caster's power through an invulnerable body. Both Syrene and Satanis sought out Superman for their purposes and, in the ensuing battle, Syrene was apparently destroyed. Satanis recovered the runestone but, before he could complete the ritual, Syrene returned from Limbo. Syrene sent the runestone further into the past to thwart Lord Satanis and buy herself time.

Lord Satanis located the stone again but, before he could obtain it, he was banished to Hell by Syrene. Syrene took her time preparing the ritual of the runestone; she assumed Satanis would not return, but she underestimated her new husband. Satanis made a deal with the Lord of Hell and was returned to the 14th Century, where he summoned both Superman and the runestone. Before he could complete the ritual and filter the runestone's power through Superman, Syrene arrived and, in the ensuing battle, Superman was split into two individuals. Each of the "Supermen" possessed only half of the number of powers of the original.

Syrene grabbed the invulnerable Superman and departed, taking the runestone with her. Satanis dispatched the now-useless Superman in his possession back to his proper time. He first took the precaution of reading Superman's mind, and using his magic, barred every means of time travel that Superman knew of.

Lord Satanis found Syrene in the act of filtering the runestone's power through the invulnerable Superman, but Syrene kept Satanis at bay until she could complete the ceremony. The invulnerable Superman, drained by the ordeal, died.

Syrene tried to dispatch her husband with the runestone's power, but Satanis thwarted her by merging with the body of the dead Superman. With Superman's powers supplementing his own, Satanis fought Syrene and seemingly killed her. However, Superman's reawakening consciousness altered Satanis' death spell and returned Syrene to her own time.

At this point, the other Superman, who had obtained the use of Rip Hunter's Time Sphere, arrived to confront Satanis and rejoin his other "half". The mind of the Superman that Lord Satanis possessed rebelled against the mage, who was forced to split. When the two Supermen touched, the runestone's residual magicks recombined them into one, complete Superman. Overwhelming Satanis, Superman knocked him back to his own time, hoping he and Syrene would keep each other occupied. Neither has been heard of since.

METHODS

Despite their similarities (or because of them), Lord Satanis and Syrene were continually at war with each other once the chance of obtaining the runestone was present. Each of them planned to use it to make him or herself the most powerful sorcerer of all time and to destroy the other.

With the runestone no longer available, the pair will probably seek other means to enhance their power. It is not certain what the victor's goals will be once his/her rival is destroyed. It is unlikely either one would content him/herself with the rule of just one planet.

Both Satanis and Syrene possess an almost unlimited array of spells, none of which they have ever used more than once. Each has the knowledge to use his/her abilities to best advantage in a particular situation.

ROLE-PLAYING

Both Syrene and Lord Satanis are totally ruthless in their quest for power. It is likely that Syrene remained allied with her father, Ambra, during the rebellion more out of fear of his powers than any filial love. It is not known what the fate of the sorcerers who allied themselves with Satanis is, but it is likely that they were killed once Syrene and Satanis assumed the throne.

Lord Satanis is evidently a megalomaniac; he swears humiliation, destruction, and utter annihilation on his opponents with every other breath. Syrene is just as harsh; she is merely less vocal about her feelings.

Satanis and Syrene have neither compassion nor any other redeeming human qualities. When Lord Satanis was sent to 14th-Century Earth, battered and beaten by Satan, he was nursed back to health by friendly peasants. He returned their kindness by slaughtering the entire village when his health was restored. He also used Lois Lane as a hostage to force Superman's hand; he has taken great delight in toying with Superman on numerous occasions. Although Syrene's role during much of this has been passive, her few appearances give evidence that she would have reacted in much the same way.

METALLO *alias Roger Corben*

DEX:	9	STR:	9	BODY:	9
INT:	5	WILL:	5	MIND:	5
INFL:	5	AURA:	3	SPIRIT:	4
INITIATIVE:	19	HERO POINTS:	90		
CHARGES:	60				
COST:	944 HPs + $ 510K				

POWERS:

Invulnerability: 12, Regeneration, 8, Skin Armor: 11

SKILLS:

Gadgetry: 6, Thief/Security Systems: 5, Vehicles/Air and Land: 6

LIMITATIONS:

Sensory Limitation: No sense of touch

CONNECTIONS:

Metropolis Underworld (high-level)

MOTIVATION: Psychopathic

WEALTH: Affluent

JOB: Professional Criminal

RACE: Artificial Life (cyborg)

EQUIPMENT:

JET SCOOTER

DEX:	0	STR:	4	BODY:	8
CHARGES:	15				
COST:	169 HPs + $ 4K				

POWERS:
Flight: 8

While Metallo would be a formidable foe against most opponents because of his robotic body, his strength is inconsequential next to that of Superman's. Despite this, Metallo is a member of Superman's Rogues Gallery because of his Kryptonite heart.

BACKGROUND

John Corben, Roger's brother, was the first Metallo. Crushed in an accident, his body was replaced with a humanoid machine form. John then became a powered criminal; he was opposed by Superman and died while trying to replenish his power source with Kryptonite.

When Roger heard of his brother's death, he swore revenge and joined SKULL. He was caught in a crossfire between Superman, the Atomic Skull, and his fellow SKULL operatives and was crushed by a ceiling cave-in.

The cave-in was not an accident, but a SKULL set-up. SKULL took Corben and transplanted his head onto a mechanical body similar to his deceased brother's. Unlike John's body, SKULL used artificial Kryptonite (later replaced by real Kryptonite) to power Roger's cybernetic body.

At first Roger worked for SKULL. He was forced to fake his own death at the end of his first battle against Superman. Roger uncovered SKULL's duplicity in his creation and swore revenge on SKULL and Superman.

Since then, Metallo has been involved in numerous operations against Superman, SKULL, the scientists who created him, and S.T.A.R. Labs. He needs to find more Kryptonite, as the power requirements of his body use up Kryptonite radiation at an incredible rate. Despite his Kryptonite heart, Superman has always been able to get the best of Metallo. In a recent raid on S.T.A.R. Labs, he met defeat at the hands of the Blue Devil, who ripped out his Kryptonite heart.

METHODS

To his credit, Metallo's plots have never been as simple as "Stand over Superman and poison him to death." He is an intricate schemer and knows enough to use mercenary henchmen. His robot body makes him more than a match for most other heroes.

Although he is no scientist, Metallo has learned quite a bit about the workings of his own body. He has experimented with a number of alternate power sources, including a form of Kryptonite that affects less molecularly dense humanoids, and a piece of dwarf star material. Any crime Metallo commits at this time will probably be aimed at finding a stable, readily available power source for himself, and from there going on to destroy SKULL and Superman.

ROLE-PLAYING

Corben is driven by hatred: hatred of Superman, hatred of SKULL, and hatred of his freak status. In the past he has shown no hesitation about slaughtering anyone who stood in his way. He seeks power because there is nothing else left to him; he feels he has been deprived of all the pleasures of life. Unlike heroes such as Cyborg and Robotman, he has not risen above his situation.

No matter how great his hatred of his freak status, Metallo's sense of self-preservation is greater. If he were to obtain all of his immediate goals, there would be little left for him. He would probably attempt to reduce others to the same semi-human status as himself out of hatred for humanity. Metallo is far too shortsighted to even dream of ruling the world or display any other form of Power Lust.

BLACKROCK *alias Dr. Peter Silverstone*

DEX:	15	STR:	3	BODY:	6
INT:	6	WILL:	5	MIND:	7
INFL:	3	AURA:	2	SPIRIT:	3
INITIATIVE:	24	HERO POINTS:	140		

EQUIPMENT:

POWER STONE

DEX:	0	STR:	0	BODY:	5
INT:	0	WILL:	0	MIND:	0
CHARGES:	EPS **				
COST:	5844 HPs + $ 119B				

POWERS:

Force Field: 35, Illusion: 14, Lightning*: 36, Teleportation: 29

* Power comes from non-Mystical source.

** **Restriction:** Power Stone may only be used in areas where broadcast frequencies can be picked up.

SKILLS:

Gadgetry: 12, Scholar/Academic Study (Electronics): 18, Scientist: 14

CONNECTIONS:

United Broadcasting Company (low-level)

MOTIVATION: Mercenary

WEALTH: Affluent

JOB:

Director of Research & Development at UBC, now professional criminal

RACE: Human

Dr. Silverstone is motivated by the need to meet a challenge as well as by the prospect of monetary gain.

Silverstone's many operations in Metropolis have brought him into conflict with Superman on a number of occasions.

BACKGROUND

Dr. Silverstone was in charge of Research & Development at United Broadcasting Company when its president, Samuel Tanner, came to him and ordered him to create a hero for UBC to exploit; Tanner felt that WGBS had gained its many exclusives with Superman in the same way.

Silverstone, who had helped invent color television, the long-playing record, and America's first communications satellite, was intrigued by the challenge of generating a hero. He used his scientific expertise to design a wand resembling a television antenna that could channel broadcast waves into incalculable power. Having no desire to confront Superman himself, Silverstone hypnotized Tanner into becoming "Blackrock" (the nickname of the UBC building).

For all of Blackrock's powers, he didn't have a chance of winning the super-ratings war against Superman. So Silverstone restored Tanner's mental faculties, leaving no memory of his Blackrock career.

Later, Silverstone created a more powerful, albeit experimental, focus for his creation, a black fist-sized power stone which could be strapped to a person's palm. When UBC's ratings slipped months later, Blackrock reappeared. Silverstone had hypnotized Tanner's nephew, comedian Les Vegas, into becoming Blackrock this time. The power stone caused Superman and Blackrock to switch identities temporarily. Afterwards, Superman easily defeated his airwave rival.

The third time Silverstone needed Blackrock, he used a construct of charged ions to animate the Blackrock suit. Superman again emerged triumphant. It was Supergirl who finally captured Silverstone when he donned the Blackrock costume himself in an attempt at industrial espionage. He is currently imprisoned at a low-security federal installation.

METHODS

As the wearer of the Blackrock suit was usually a hypnotized pawn, its user rarely displayed much imagination in the use of his powers. In public, Blackrock would play the hero, never endangering passersby or

47

doing anything that would make him unpopular. In private, Blackrock ruthlessly sought to best Superman in direct combat.

ROLE-PLAYING

Should Dr. Silverstone ever reactivate Blackrock, he would continue to learn from past errors. Silverstone is not a ruthless, hardened criminal. However, he would do anything short of murder to continue his research in electronics.

Two difficulties that Silverstone has encountered so far with Blackrock are a lack of hand-to-hand proficiency and the sluggishness of a controlled or hypnotized mind. Silverstone is attempting to solve these problems. The power stone is still experimental. With or without Silverstone's genius, some random side-effect (such as the identity-switch mentioned above) would probably occur if it were used again. This would give Blackrock an additional power or two.

MASTER JAILER	*alias Carl Draper*	
DEX: 9	STR: 4	BODY: 6
INT: 8	WILL: 7	MIND: 8
INFL: 4	AURA: 3	SPIRIT: 4
INITIATIVE: 21 (24)	HERO POINTS: 125	

SKILLS:
Detective/Clue Analysis, ID Systems and Police Procedures: 6, Gadgetry: 14, Martial Artist/Attack Advantage: 3, Military Science/Camouflage and ECM: 9, Scholar/Academic Study (Escapology): 18, Scientist/Drawing Plans: 7, Thief/Escape Artist, Locks and Safes, Security Systems, and Stealth: 11

LIMITATIONS:
● Catastrophic Irrational Attraction: Jails and Traps
● Miscellaneous Limitation: has a -4 Column Shift to his OV for designing jails and traps, but a +4 Column Shift to his OV on any other use of his Gadgetry Skill

MOTIVATION: Mercenary
WEALTH: Comfortable
JOB: Professional Criminal
RACE: Human
EQUIPMENT:

JAILER SUIT		
DEX: 0	STR: 0	BODY: 12
CHARGES: NA		
COST: 192 HPs + $ 60K		

6 OMNI-GADGETS	
CLASS A:	5
CLASS B:	4
CLASS C:	5
CHARGES:	NA
COST: *HPs + $ 700	

The Master Jailer is the greatest prison designer and one of the greatest escape artists of the 20th Century. Unfortunately, the events which shaped him into such an individual have also made him a formidable opponent of Superman.

BACKGROUND

Carl "Moosie" Draper was a pudgy, somewhat homely child. He was a peer of Clark Kent at Smallville High. Although Carl was not too bright, he had a knack for designing and figuring out traps. He also suffered from a crush on Lana Lang. When Carl and Lana's class was caught in a cave-in during a school outing, he found a way out and returned to the group, only to be upstaged when Superboy saved the class.

Still crazy about Lana, Draper followed her career after she graduated. He also undertook a regimen of physical exercise, plastic surgery, and study in order to, in his words, escape the prison that Nature made of his body. He became a master architect and locksmith. Time and again he tried to prove himself superior to Superman and to win the attention of Lana Lang. He believed that by designing a prison to permanently hold Superman's archfoes, he would earn Lana's affection.

Draper was upstaged again when Superman stationed the prison 20,000 feet in the air with anti-gravity mechanisms and sealed it with an impenetrable dome. To revenge himself, Draper swore took the identity of the Master Jailer. Kidnapping Lana, he captured and trapped Superman in the supposedly inescapable "Eternity Trap." Lana scorned Draper's attentions and gave Superman an

opportunity to escape and apprehend Draper.

No prison, even his own, could hold Draper. Since his escape, he has hired himself out to a group that wanted Supergirl out of the way, but she managed to escape two of his traps. He has also resorted to robbery to finance his traps, which he views as not only functional but artistic.

METHODS

As he has no powers and rarely uses devices to enhance his own capacities, the Master Jailer rarely confronts his foes directly. He prefers to surprise and ensnare his victim in a trap with all of the prisoner's Limitations and Vulnerabilities in mind. Draper will use advanced weaponry if necessary, but he will not indulge in extended firefights.

The Master Jailer's traps are always intricate, but they are not fool-proof. His prisoners have yet to circumvent him, but they usually take advantage of some surprise element of which Draper is not aware.

ROLE-PLAYING

Draper is, in some ways, the typical Superman foe. He is a man with no natural powers, but he has scientific skills and a motif; he also possesses some mental problems.

Draper's psyche still bears the scars of his childhood. His love of Lana Lang seems to have been transferred to expressing artistry through his traps, and he has made no further romantic overtures. His hatred is not aimed at society per se, but at heroes like Superman who upstage him as he was upstaged by Superboy as a child.

KARB-BRAK	*alias Andrew Meda*	
DEX: 20	STR: 45	BODY: 50
INT: 10	WILL: 12	MIND: 20
INFL: 5	AURA: 5	SPIRIT: 5
INITIATIVE: 35	HERO POINTS: 130	

POWERS:
Bomb: 35, Flight: 45, Invulnerability: 50, Recall: 20, Sealed Systems: 20, Superspeed: 25, Systemic Antidote: 20, X-Ray Vision: 20

SKILLS:
Gadgetry: 8, Vehicles: 6

VULNERABILITIES:

Rare Fatal Vulnerability:
Kryptonian powered individuals
Range: 4 APs

MOTIVATION: NA
WEALTH: NA
JOB: NA
RACE: Alien

Karb-Brak, an alien from the Andromeda galaxy, is fatally allergic to all individuals with powers. As such, he can be one of Superman's most dangerous foes because he fights for neither personal gain nor revenge: he fights for his life.

BACKGROUND

On Karb-Brak's homeworld everyone had powers; it was these same abilities which triggered Karb-Brak's allergic reaction. After his people searched scores of galaxies, they found an ideal place for Karb-Brak: Earth. He arrived with a handful of super-scientific gadgets from his native planet and assumed the human guise of Andrew Meda.

Unfortunately, Superman's Kryptonian physiognomy was similar enough to that of Karb-Brak's own people to trigger the allergic reaction. Although Superman once used the medical equipment of his Fortress of Solitude to effect a cure for Karb-Brak's condition, the allergic fever returned months later. Karb-Brak is currently enjoying a long remission of his allergy and is at home in the Andromeda Galaxy.

METHODS

Normally Karb-Brak's powers would not be a match for Superman's, but the pasty-skinned alien has several advantages over the Man of Steel. First, his allergic condition is contagious. If Karb-Brak and Superman come within 4 APs of each other, they both acquire symptoms. In Karb-Brak's case, the result is loss of BODY APs. However, the fever causes physical weakness and an increase in body temperature to Superman. This causes all of Superman's Physical Attributes and Powers to decrease by 5 APs.

Secondly, Karb-Brak has access to super-scientific equipment from his homeworld. Among these tools is his Psi-machine, which was originally an entertainment device. He has altered Superman's memories with this device, as well as the memories of the entire population of Metropolis. He has also sent Superman back 200 years to colonial America. The Gamemaster may choose other devices to give Karb-Brak, bearing in mind that few would actually be weapons, but each could be modified to cause Superman discomfort in some way.

Thirdly, Karb-Brak's feverish desperation sometimes works to his advantage. When trying to eliminate Superman, Karb-Brak is ruthless and unconcerned about innocents. During battles with Karb-Brak, Superman can be distracted by the need to protect both innocents and his secret identity. Karb-Brak willingly expends large amounts of Hero Points when attacking the Man of Tomorrow.

ROLE-PLAYING

Kark-Brak is not evil, but he is ruthless, selfish, and arrogant. If he suffers another relapse he will return to Earth, the only suitable planet he knows. And he will probably be better prepared to eliminate Superman's presence, possibly with Gold Kryptonite or machinery as advanced as his Psi-machine.

Coincidentally, each time Karb-Brak's fever has flared, other heroes (and villains) to whom he might be allergic, such as Supergirl or the Phantom Zone villains, have not been on Earth; Karb-Brak is presumably not aware of their existence. If the Phantom Zoners were on Earth during one of Karb-Brak's visits, the Andromedan might conceivably ally with Superman to defeat them, as he has no desire to see Earth destroyed.

ATOMIC SKULL *alias Dr. Albert Michaels*					
DEX:	9	STR:	3	BODY:	5
INT:	7	WILL:	5	MIND:	6
INFL:	5	AURA:	2	SPIRIT:	4
INITIATIVE:	21		HERO POINTS:	100	

POWERS:
Mental Blast: 36

SKILLS:
Charisma: 7, Scientist: 10

LIMITATIONS:
Power Limitation: Must have hands free to use his Mental Blast Power

VULNERABILITIES:

Miscellaneous Vulnerability:
Must use his Mental Blast Power at least once every 4 hours (12 APs). Otherwise, his MIND is reduced to -6, with only Resting Recovery allowed.

MOTIVATION: Power Lust
WEALTH: Comfortable
JOB: Professional Criminal
RACE: Human

Once a respected scientist, the Atomic Skull is now a tragic figure who has been driven to crime by the neural disorder that gives him his Mental Blast Power.

BACKGROUND

Dr. Albert Michaels was the director of S.T.A.R. Labs and has had dozens of inventions patented. When he was stricken with a terminal neural disorder, Michaels traded his inventions to SKULL in return for a neural pacemaker. The pacemaker eventually malfunctioned, turning his brainwaves into a new form of energy that could be projected as potent energy blasts.

With all his bridges burned behind him, Dr. Michaels took control of SKULL. He led the organization against Superman, but several defeats caused dissatisfaction among the group and he was expelled. Since then, he has had no choice but to act as a professional criminal.

METHODS

The Atomic Skull is not particularly subtle, although he doesn't need to be when his Mental Blast Power can overcome Superman with relative ease. His crimes are usually thefts of valuable technology.

ROLE-PLAYING

Michaels is a driven man. He was forced to betray his S.T.A.R. Labs position to gain any hope of a cure. Therefore, crime is the only real occupation left to him. Although he has gained some control over the Mental Blast Power in recent years, he must still periodically discharge the energy before his brain burns out (as per Vulnerability). He blames Superman for his past defeats and his current condition.

container. A plant growth stimulant failure apparently acted as a catalyst and animated the chemicals and container into some bizarre, malevolent life form. Chemo, as Norton called the container, killed the Professor and went on a mindless wave of devastation, only to be stopped by the Metal Men.

Although Chemo was apparently destroyed, the dispersed chemicals eventually coalesced into their humanoid form, and have done so many times since. After a battle with the Metal Men and Superman in Metropolis, the chemical monstrosity has fixated on that city.

METHODS

Chemo has one tactic: spraying acid at anything that moves. Chemo's other specialty is reanimating from absolute obliteration.

ROLE-PLAYING

Chemo is totally mindless, with an understandable lack of personality. His sheer witlessness makes him an excellent pawn for more intelligent villains, but most sophisticated villains like Luthor and Brainiac prefer their own, more reliable devices.

PARASITE *alias Raymond Maxwell*					
DEX:	7	STR:	3	BODY:	6
INT:	4	WILL:	5	MIND:	3
INFL:	5	AURA:	3	SPIRIT:	3
INITIATIVE:	16			HERO POINTS:	110

POWERS:
Adaptation: 80, Mind Drain: 20, Power Drain: 30, Spiritual Drain: 20, Vampirism: 20

SKILLS:
Vehicles/Land: 3

LIMITATIONS:
- Can only use Adaptation to gain Powers and Attributes of Characters within 2 APs. Loses 4 APs of the acquired Power or Attribute per phase thereafter.
- Powers acquired through Power Drain may only be retained for 2 APs of time.
- Power Limitation: Powers and Attributes may only be drained from living beings.
- Catastrophic Irrational Attraction: Needs to feel energy

from acquired Powers flow through him.

VULNERABILITIES
Common Miscellaneous Vulnerability:
Acquires all Limitations and Vulnerabilities of Powers taken from another Character.

MOTIVATION: Psychopathic
WEALTH: Struggling
JOB: Professional Criminal
RACE: Human

The Parasite is a major threat to Superman due to his uncanny ability to siphon off Superman's powers and use them against him.

BACKGROUND

Maxwell Jensen, who was unable to keep a job for any length of time, obtained work at a government lab as a handyman. Assuming that the lab was storing payrolls in radiation-proof canisters he pried one open, receiving a faceful of radiation for his efforts. Hideously disfigured, Jensen took the name of the Parasite after he discovered his ability to absorb the mental and physical essence of any other being. Seeking as much power as possible, he battled Superman and was defeated.

After years of defeats, the Parasite lost his powers, married, and had twins. However, an alien being named Xavier gathered together a group of Superman's foes and restored Jensen's power. Jensen then became a threat to his loved ones once again.

METHODS

Jensen relies on his power-draining abilities almost entirely. However, he has devised a number of means of getting close enough to the Man of Tomorrow to drain his powers to the utmost. In one of his last battles with Superman, the Parasite was exposed to Gold Kryptonite, but it is not clear if he can absorb a new dose of Superman's abilities.

ROLE-PLAYING

Jensen hungers for powers flowing through his body, but he also feels the pain and frustration of being unable

---

CHEMO					
DEX:	2	STR:	12	BODY:	60
INT:	1	WILL:	15	MIND:	59
INFL:	1	AURA:	2	SPIRIT:	30
INITIATIVE:	4			HERO POINTS:	65

POWERS:
Acid: 27, Growth: 7, Invulnerability: 65, Split: 5

MOTIVATION: NA
WEALTH: NA
JOB: NA
RACE: Artificial Life

Despite his lack of intelligence, Chemo is a major threat to both Superman and the world in general due to his sheer indestructability.

BACKGROUND

Chemo is the creation of Professor Ramsey Norton, a scientist who poured his failed chemical experiments into a 25' man-shaped plastic to enjoy the simple pleasures of life. He is also unhappy because he cannot meet with his wife and children.

The Parasite has a contempt for most people other than his family.

TITANO

DEX:	7	STR:	10	BODY:	16
INT:	1	WILL:	5	MIND:	5
INFL:	2	AURA:	1	SPIRIT:	5
INITIATIVE:	10	HERO POINTS:	125		

POWERS:
Bio-Energy Blast: 2, Growth: 12

NOTE: Titano's bio-energy eyebeam blasts are Green Kryptonite-based

SKILLS:
Acrobatics/Climbing: 8

LIMITATIONS:
Growth always on

MOTIVATION: NA
WEALTH: NA
JOB: NA
RACE: Mutated Animal

BACKGROUND

Originally a circus chimpanzee named Toto, Titano was sent up in a satellite for a week. The satellite was bombarded with radiation from two colliding meteors: one of uranium and one of Kryptonite. Emerging from the satellite upon its landing, Toto grew to giant size and fixated on Lois Lane. Flying to her rescue, Superman was struck down by Toto's new power, Green Kryptonite Bio-Energy Blast. Lois redubbed the giant-sized ape Titano; she used the ape's ability to mimic others to get him to don a pair of lead spectacles.

Throughout the years Titano has kept returning, most recently teleported from a planet of giants by the Atomic Skull.

METHODS & ROLE-PLAYING

Titano is usually docile and fun-loving but, like Bizarro, his mindlessness frequently makes him a danger due to his random acts.

VANDAL SAVAGE

DEX:	8	STR:	5	BODY:	9
INT:	12	WILL:	14	MIND:	16
INFL:	9	AURA:	7	SPIRIT:	10
INITIATIVE:	29 (37)	HERO POINTS:	130		

POWERS:
Invulnerability: 30

SKILLS: (* linked)
Charisma*: 9, Detective*: 12, Martial Artist*: 8, Military Science*: 12, Occultist: 4, Scholar*: 12 (all eras of History, Political Science, Psychology, Sociology, plus all Language Groups), Scientist: 6, Spy*: 12

MOTIVATION: Power Lust
WEALTH: Multimillionaire
JOB: Businessman
RACE: Human

BACKGROUND

Savage's Invulnerability has the effect of preventing him from aging. His physical appearance has not radically changed since he gained immortality 50,000 years ago.

Vandal Savage's origin can be found in the annals of prehistory, when the leader of a tribe of Cro-Magnons, Vandar Adg, met his mortal enemy in combat. Their fight was interrupted by a meteor hurtling out of the sky and exploding. Vandar Adg was exposed to the gas from the meteor and collapsed. He recovered several days later and discovered that he was virtually immortal: he could recover instantly from any mortal wound, and he never aged.

Vandar Adg led his tribe of barbarians on a number of conquests; he survived through the centuries. Vandar has claimed to be such individuals as Gilgamesh, Cheops, Julius Caesar, and Genghis Khan, although his statements have never been fully proven.

By the 1940's Vandal Savage, as the Cro-Magnon now called himself, had grown tired of life and found relief from his boredom in the game of political power. He allied himself with Hitler. Savage then opposed the Justice Society of America as a member of the Injustice Society of the World. After being released from prison years later, Savage battled the Flashes of Earth 1 and 2, but was defeated again.

Discovering a means of crossing from his native Earth-2 to Earth-1, Savage set himself up as a businessman and made an attempt to alter the past and make himself absolute ruler of the world. When this plan was foiled, he tried to defeat Earth-1's greatest champion, Superman, by striking at his Achilles' heel: his adoring public.

Savage underwent a systematic campaign to cause Superman to become scorned by the populace of Metropolis, matching his ageless cunning against Superman's brawn. His scheme went well for a time, but was ultimately foiled when the Man of Tomorrow tricked him into revealing his plan to discredit Superman on national television. Savage fled the scene before the authorities could arrive.

Vandal Savage has been at large until recently, when the new (Wally West) Flash encountered him. Savage had fatally beaten a private investigator who had discovered that Savage was living under the alias of Varney Sack.

METHODS

Although Vandal Savage does not age and can recover from most fatal wounds, he is not a true "immortal"; it is likely he could be destroyed by decapitation or complete molecular dispersal.

Because of this, Vandal has become an expert at behind-the-scene scheming rather than direct confrontation, as there is a chance he could be accidentally killed. Within a timeframe of centuries, he has put his vast experience to work to accumulate vast wealth. In his campaign against Superman, he was never in any danger of damage or exposure. It was not until his overconfidence led him to boasting of his scheme that he was exposed to the people of Metropolis as something other than a selfless benefactor.

ROLE-PLAYING

Vandal Savage is the ultimate schemer. Although he has indulged in direct battles in the past, he will not do so now except if he has no other choice. His only mistake in his campaign against Superman was in underestimating the Man of Steel's intellect. It is likely he will return to seek vengeance on Superman, and this time it is unlikely he will allow his ego to get the better of him again.

AMAZO

DEX:	26	STR:	50	BODY:	40
INT:	5	WILL:	9	MIND:	16
INFL:	8	AURA:	14	SPIRIT:	10
INITIATIVE:	39		HERO POINTS:	180

POWERS:

Air Control: 15, Animal Control: 15, Animal Summoning: 12, Directional Hearing: 10, Extended Hearing: 10, Flight: 45, Gliding: 12, Heat Vision: 30, Jumping: 10, Microscopic Vision: 15, Running: 22, Sealed Systems: 20, Shrinking: 15, Sonic Beam: 8, Speak with Animals: 8, Stretching: 13, Superspeed: 28, Super Breath: 20, Super Hearing: 10, Super Ventriloquism: 15, Systemic Antidote: 20, Telekinesis: 7 *(Lasso only)*, Telescopic Vision: 15, Thermal Vision: 15, Ultra Vision: 7, Water Freedom: 8, X-Ray Vison: 20 *Mystic Link*: Air Control: 12, Earth Control: 12, Flame Control: 12, Flame Project: 6, Fog: 12, Ice Control: 12, Lightning: 12, Plant Control: 12, Water Control: 12, Weather Control: 12

SKILLS:

Acrobatics/Diving: 6, Detective: 12, Weaponry: 7

LIMITATIONS:

- Animal Powers work only on marine life.
- Ring's Force Manipulation is ineffective against anything colored yellow.
- All Mystically Linked Powers are spells, which must be spoken backwards to use.

MOTIVATION: NA

WEALTH: NA

JOB: NA

RACE: Artificial Life (robotic android)

EQUIPMENT:

LASSO

DEX:	0	STR:	20	BODY:	35
INT:	0	WILL:	0	MIND:	0
CHARGES:	15				
COST:	3436 HPs + $ 32.5B				

POWERS:

Control: 10

POWER RING

DEX:	0	STR:	0	BODY:	20
INT:	0	WILL:	0	MIND:	0
CHARGES:	20				
COST:			HPs + $ 850B		

POWERS:

Flight: 40, Force Manipulation: 25

Aptly described as the "One-Man Justice League," Amazo is one of the most powerful villains on Earth.

BACKGROUND

The android Amazo is the creation of Professor Ivo, a scientist who devised him as a weapon to oppose the Justice League. The android's special absorption cells allowed him to gain the powers of all of the members of the original Justice League and, armed with a duplicate Green Lantern power ring and a duplicate of Wonder Woman's lasso, he almost proved to be a match for the JLA. Green Lantern was able to use the android's inability to use the power ring on the color yellow to defeat him.

Amazo was kept sealed in a glass cylinder in the JLA's Trophy Room for many years. Despite the android's professed desire for the electronic "sleep of oblivion" he was reactivated time after time, either by Ivo or one of the League's other foes.

Amazo had been scrapped and left in orbit around the Earth when a wave of red sun radiation swept the Earth and reactivated him. He sought Professor Ivo, who had apparently reformed and was teaching college. Amazo believed that Ivo summoned him. Superman, weakened by the same radiation responsible for Amazo's reawakening, attempted to protect Ivo and was able to delay the android long enough for the wave of radiation to pass.

The mechanical monstrosity was defeated and returned to his electronic sleep, it seemed for good. Unfortunately, the immortality serum that Ivo had taken many years before caused him to mutate into a hideously deformed freak. Needing the life force of one man — Superman — to restore him to normal, Professor Ivo reactivated Amazo yet again and used him to attempt to lure the Man of Tomorrow into a trap. Superman saw

through the ruse and defeated Amazo once more. It is extremely likely that Ivo will reactivate his creation again.

METHODS

Amazo possesses the powers of every Justice Leaguer he has encountered, giving him the combined powers of Aquaman, Atom, Batman, Black Canary, Elongated Man, Flash, Green Lantern, Red Tornado, Superman, Wonder Woman and Zatanna. With so much sheer power at his command, Amazo has never been defeated in direct combat. Only through trickery has Superman and the Justice League ever subdued him.

Amazo originally had some trouble controlling all of his powers; he was only able to use the abilities of one hero at a time, but he has since mastered the art of using more than one power simultaneously. He is quite good at mixing and matching powers to his advantage.

ROLE-PLAYING

Amazo is an android, albeit one possessed of a high level of sentience. He reacts in a totally logical way to most situations: it is usually the illogical desires of his programmers that cause him to act in other than a totally mechanical manner.

BLACKBRIAR THORN

DEX:	5	STR:	4	BODY:	9
INT:	11	WILL:	14	MIND:	11
INFL:	13	AURA:	17	SPIRIT:	16
INITIATIVE:	29		HERO POINTS:	135

POWERS:

Air Control: 14, Earth Control: 14, Flame Control: 14, Flame Immunity: 6, Flame Project: 7, Fog: 16, Illusions: 12, Magical Sense: 5, Lightning: 7, Plant Control: 14, Plant Growth: 17, Skin Armor: 9, Suspension: 35, Water Control: 14, Weather Control: 17

SKILLS:

Charisma/Intimidation: 6, Occultist/Identify Object: 8

LIMITATIONS:

Miscellaneous Limitation: Unfamiliarity with 20th Century.

VULNERABILITIES:

Loss Vulnerability — all Powers: must maintain contact with the earth

MOTIVATION: Power Lust
WEALTH: NA
JOB: NA
RACE: Human

Blackbriar Thorn has opposed Superman on at least one occasion. His Mystical Powers make him a tough opponent for the Man of Tomorrow.

BACKGROUND

Thorn was the high priest of one of several Druidic sects in the British Isles. He reigned supreme for many years until the Romans came to the Isles and wiped out all traces of the so-called heretical religious practices of the Druids.

Thorn was forced to flee for his life. Chased by Roman legionnaires, he slipped into the nearby woods and transformed himself into a wooden statue to elude pursuit. The ruse worked, but his fellow Druids unleashed an earthquake in their death-throes. In the resulting cataclysm Thorn was swallowed up by a fissure.

For many years Thorn remained buried in a form of suspended animation. He was eventually discovered during an excavation by Professor Lewis Lang, who was researching the ancient Druidic cults. The "statue" was brought to Gotham City by Professor Lang and put on display. After being exposed to full moonlight for the first time since his entombment, Thorn's residual magical energies acted to revive him. Although he remained enshrouded in wood, he was otherwise unimpaired both physically and mystically.

Unfamiliar with his surroundings, Thorn went on a rampage; he attempted to restore Gotham City to a natural, overgrown state. Fortunately, both Clark Kent and Jason Blood, famed demonologist and occult researcher, were on hand. As Superman and the Demon Etrigan, they battled Thorn and were ultimately able to defeat him by uprooting him from the ground and carrying him high into the air. He was apparently destroyed when his powers failed him; no trace of him was found.

METHODS

Blackbriar Thorn is a master of the elements and possesses other mystical abilities as well. He was one of the most skilled conjurers of his day and has retained his full magical abilities and knowledge throughout his long imprisonment.

In combat, Thorn will use his magical abilities to his best advantage. He will direct the full fury of the elements at anyone unwise enough to cross him.

ROLE-PLAYING

Blackbriar Thorn is essentially a man out of his time. He has little understanding of the 20th Century and considers most heroes "fellow demons." When he was in Gotham City he had two desires, to cause the plants to overgrow the city and to trade his body for Superman's.

Thorn is uncomfortable with technology and prefers surroundings in a wild and natural state. If he returned, he would still probably seek out Superman to make a body transfer.

COLONEL FUTURE		*alias Col. Edmond Hamilton*
DEX: 5	STR: 2	BODY: 5
INT: 6	WILL: 8	MIND: 5
INFL: 4	AURA: 3	SPIRIT: 3
INITIATIVE: 15 (20)		HERO POINTS: 160

POWERS:

Precognition: 15, Recall: 13

SKILLS: (* *linked*)

Gadgetry: 6, Martial Artist/Attack Advantage & Taking a Blow*: 5, Military Science: 5, Scientist: 8, Weaponry: 7

LIMITATIONS:

- Flight — Minor chance of failure. Roll 2D10 once every two phases that the rocket pack is in use; must roll a 7 or greater in order for the pack's Flight to work. If the roll fails, the rocket pack cannot be used for another four phases.
- Precognition will only function in a critical life-or-death situation (GM's discretion). In compensation, he does not have to be touching a person or object to see their future.
- Precognition's subject is chosen randomly by the Gamemaster.
- Telekinesis can only be used to immobilize an opponent.

MOTIVATION: NA
WEALTH: Affluent
JOB: Director at NASA
RACE: Human
EQUIPMENT:

BATTLE SUIT		
DEX: 20	STR: 0	BODY: 17
INT: 0	WILL: 0	MIND: 0
CHARGES: 28		
COST: 1450 HPs + $ 63M		

POWERS:

Force Field: 15, Warp: 11

ROCKET PACK		
DEX: 0	STR: 0	BODY: 7
CHARGES: 13		
COST: 181 HPs + $ 20K		

POWERS:

Flight: 10 (see *Limitations*)

WEAPON BELT		
DEX: 0	STR: 0	BODY: 6
INT: 0	WILL: 0	MIND: 0
CHARGES: 23		
COST: 3798 HPs + $ 610B		

POWERS:

Telekinesis: 40, Teleportation: 10, Digging: 5

SPECIAL: Colonel Future adds the APs of his Battle Suit's Warp to his Initiative during phases in which he uses his battle suit's Warp Power.

Although Colonel Future is not a true villain, he has clashed with Superman on at least two occasions, and he might possibly return.

BACKGROUND

Edmond Hamilton is a talented inventor who is fascinated by science, technology, and the future. Hamilton is gifted at adapting existing technology to new uses, and he rose quickly through the U.S. Air Force ranks. He was transferred to NASA, where he became head of NASA's Future Planning Section.

Due to a freak electrical accident, Hamilton found himself capable of predicting the future. Unfortunately, he also found that his Precognition Power only works when his life is threatened. During the accident, he caught a glimpse of a catastrophe which destroyed Earth.

Colonel Hamilton set up a device that could put his life in danger under controlled conditions; he was thus able to gain more glimpses into the future. Duplicating the technology which he saw, he created special equipment which would allow him to prevent the foreseen disaster. His efforts brought him into conflict with Superman. The two battled briefly before Superman was able to ascertain that the disaster Hamilton had seen was, in fact, an event of the Man of Tomorrow's own making, which Colonel Future had misread.

Hamilton then retired as Colonel Future. However, he later caught a glimpse of another future in which Superman was killed. He donned his gear to prevent Superman's death, only to discover that he had again misread his precognitive glimpse. Superman convinced Hamilton to retire Colonel Future, but, bearing in mind Hamilton's talent for going off half-cocked, it is likely he will return.

METHODS

Hamilton has spent long hours in practice with the equipment which he has designed based on his future glimpses. He can create pocket warps and duck through them so quickly as to keep ahead of Superman.

Hamilton never enters Killing Combat. In fact, he will not even enter combat at all unless forced to. Unfortunately, his future-glimpses seem to land him into situations in which he is required to confront Superman. He will never attempt to harm the Man of Tomorrow, only delay and/or incapacitate him. He would take the same attitude towards other heroes if he came into conflict with them.

ROLE-PLAYING

Although Hamilton means well, he is rather self-righteous (in a good-natured way). He always has to be forcibly convinced that he has misread the future. It is practically impossible for him to get an accurate glimpse of the future while in a life-or-death situation.

Hamilton has read lots of 40's and 50's science fiction and Flash Gordon serials; he tends to view himself in a similarly dashing way. His heroism usually goes awry, unfortunately.

J. WILBUR WOLFINGHAM

DEX:	3	STR:	2	BODY:	2
INT:	4	WILL:	2	MIND:	3
INFL:	2	AURA:	2	SPIRIT:	2
INITIATIVE:	9		HERO POINTS:	15	

SKILLS:

Charisma/Persuasion: 5, Detective/Law: 4

MOTIVATION: Greed
WEALTH: Struggling
JOB: Confidence Man
RACE: Human

A perennial conman and swindler, Wolfingham might have been a success in his chosen profession if not for Superman's frequent interventions.

BACKGROUND

Little is known of Wolfingham's background before he appeared in Metropolis with his first confidence racket. He has devised a number of ingenious scams to make money from poor unsuspecting investors through marginally legal schemes.

Unfortunately, Superman has always been around to intervene, stepping in to guarantee that Wolfingham's victims actually came out ahead and that the confidence man ends up with nothing.

PSYCHOLOGY

Wolfingham is the perfect image of a confidence swindler. His attitude is echoed by the stated philosophy of an actor of yesteryear who is his idol: "Never give a sucker an even break or wise up a chump." Ironically, Wolfingham is curiously blind to other confidence scams; he has been taken on more than one occasion.

ROLE-PLAYING

Wolfingham is not one for physical violence, being an inveterate coward. He prefers to rely on intricate, somewhat outrageous schemes. He has faith in the old adage, "There's a sucker born every minute." He is rarely wrong in his estimation of the public, but Superman's intervention guarantees that he never makes any money, either.

THE PHANTOM ZONE

ITS ORIGINS

Ages and ages ago, two spiral galaxies, each rich with hundreds of thousands of life-bearing planets, collided. Almost all of these planets perished from the resulting tidal forces. The billions and billions of minds of the planets' inhabitants — their very will to survive — lived on as the being called Aethyr.

To further insulate and protect itself, Aethyr willed itself into an other-dimensional universe; the Phantom Zone is the outermost layer of this universe. Aethyr created multiple other-dimensional layers which bounded both the limbo of the Phantom Zone and the outer reality. These realities shift constantly, as they exist at the whim of Aethyr.

ITS DISCOVERY

Approximately two years before Krypton's doom, the scientist Jor-El earned a place on the ruling Science Council by devising a humane and supposedly inescapable means of confining criminals: banishment to the wraithlike dimension which he named "The Phantom Zone." Jor-El discovered the Phantom Zone while trying to find a means of evacuating Krypton before its destruction.

During this time, Jor-El invented the Phantom Zone Projector. With the use of the Projector, dozens of criminals were successfully banished to the Zone to serve out their terms.

Unfortunately, the Phantom Zoners were able to combine their mental essences in an almost successful attempt to force Jor-El to release them. As a result of this incident, the Science Council decreed that the Zone Projector be launched into space, along with a cache of forbidden weapons that were used by Jor-El's cousin, Kru-El. Krypton was destroyed nine days later. The Projector eventually came to Earth; it has been in Superman's possession ever since.

There have been other Projectors built. One was in use in the bottle city of Kandor until the city was enlarged. Another was created by Zor-El of Argo City, but it was lost along with the domed metropolis. Both Superman and the Kandorians sentenced more Kryptonian criminals to the Zone, and they released those whose sentences had expired.

Recently, dozens of the Zone's powered criminals escaped from the Phantom Zone and managed to return to corporeal form on Earth. Over a dozen of the Zone's most deadly inhabitants exerted their combined willpower over the mind of Quex-Ul and switched places with Quex-Ul and the Man of Steel. Quex-Ul had been wrongly exiled to the Zone on a previous occasion, but was released by Superman after the Man of Steel discovered the injustice of Quex-Ul's confinement. Shortly after his release, Quex-Ul lost both his memory and powers when he exposed himself to Gold Kryptonite in order to save Superman. While in the Phantom Zone, Quex-Ul regained his memory. Unfortunately, he was forced to sacrifice his life so that Superman could escape and return the Phantom Zoners to their imprisonment.

Of the Kryptonians imprisoned in the Phantom Zone, only three have attempted to pass through the dimensions of Aethyr on their own. The first was the priest of Joru named Thul-Kar, who entered the Zone magically on Krypton's last day. For his efforts to pass through Aethyr's realm, Thul-Kar was hideously deformed and sentenced to guard one of the middle realms. The other two were Quex-Ul and Superman.

GAME MECHANICS

Any Character trapped in the

56

PHANTOM ZONE OCCUPANTS

The exact number of Phantom Zone occupants is not known; it has fluctuated as more prisoners have been sentenced to the Zone, or released by Superman or the Kandorians. None have been known to possess innate powers capable of attacking the MIND or SPIRIT. However, there is a special type of Mental attack that is dicussed in the last paragraph in this section.

All of the occupants of the Phantom Zone are criminals with the exception of Mon-El. This youth, an astronaut from the planet Daxam, was accidentally exposed to lead. Lead permanently poisons Daxamites in the same way that Kryptonite temporarily poisons Kryptonians. As such, he can never emerge from the Phantom Zone, although he is a friend of both Superboy and Superman. He will warn Kal-El of danger from the Phantom Zoners whenever possible, but they are aware of his existence and often find means of blocking his communication.

NOTE: Mon-El is fated to emerge from the Phantom Zone in the 30th Century, when a cure is discovered for his lead poisoning. Thus, he will never play a part in 20th-Century real-world adventures. Mon-El's statistics can be found in the *Legion Of Super-Heroes Sourcebook, Vol. 1.*

All of the Phantom Zone villains hate Superman with a passion, as he is the son of the scientist who crafted their imprisonment. They have sworn vengeance and have come close to success on a number of occasions.

All Phantom Zoners acquire 12 APs of Telepathy once they enter the Zone; this allows them to communicate with each other. They can also attempt to assault and take over the minds of Kryptonians outside the Zone who are particularly weak-willed, ill, or suffering from amnesia. Such an attack is treated as a use of the Control Power. It can only work on a Kryptonian of weakened mental status (GM's discretion); there is a +4 Column Shift to the victim's OV/RV due to the different dimensions. Team Attacks may be made normally.

Phantom Zone is reduced to a non-corporeal, invisible phantom. He or she does not age and cannot be damaged by any force originating in the "real" universe, whether it be Physical, Mental or Mystical.

Although the records are not totally clear, it seems that no Phantom Zoner can touch or make a Physical attack on another Phantom Zoner. A Zoner can, however, make Mental and Mystical Attacks that affect another Zoner's INT/MIND or INFL/SPIRIT. These attacks may be felt by the victim as actual physical impacts, as a Character's perceptions are altered by the twisted realities of the Phantom Zone, but damage is applied to the appropriate Attribute.

The Phantom Zone appears to an occupant as a swirling realm of purplish mists. The real world can be dimly perceived from the Phantom Zone through a Perception Check against an OV/RV of 3/3. Any Character can travel anywhere in the Phantom Zone at a Speed of 38 APs. Although Zone occupants do not age, time passes normally for them in relation to the real world.

There are only three means of going into or out of the Phantom Zone. The first is through the use of a Phantom Zone Projector. Secondly, natives of an otherdimensional world named Bgtzl, who can turn noncorporeal at will, can enter the Zone. However, the Bgtzl native attempting to enter the Zone must make a roll with his INT/WILL as the AV/EV against an OV/RV of 6/6. It should be noted that natives of Bgtzl rarely do this. Also, they will not come into contact with Earth until the 30th Century, the time of the existence of the Legion of Super-Heroes. Legionnaire Tinya Wazzo (Phantom Girl) is from Bgtzl.

The third way for a Character to enter or leave the Zone is to pass through the various levels of Aethyr. It is up to the Gamemaster as what these realms consist of, as they are subject to Aethyr's whims, but the voyager will usually have to pass through 3-5 realms with differing effects. The intrepid traveller will be subject to attacks on either his/her Mental or Mystical Attributes with an AV/EV of from 6 to 10 (Gamemaster's discretion). The Character will finally have to pass through the core of Aethyr itself, which will attack the voyager's Mystical Attributes with an AV/EV of 9/9. If the traveller remains conscious through this last attack, he/she will reemerge into the real universe.

A typical Phantom Zoner possesses the following statistics:

PHANTOM ZONER

DEX:	20	STR:	48	BODY:	36
INT:	8	WILL:	6	MIND:	10
INFL:	8	AURA:	3	SPIRIT:	3
INITIATIVE:	36	HERO POINTS:	45		

POWERS:
Directional Hearing: 10, Extended Hearing: 10, Flight: 45, Heat Vision: 30, Invulnerability: 45, Sealed Systems: 20, Solar Sustenance: 50, Super Breath: 20, Super Hearing: 10, Superspeed: 22, Systemic Antidote: 20, Telescopic Vision: 15, Thermal Vision: 15, X-Ray Vision: 20

SKILLS:
Gadgetry: 9, Scientist: 15

LIMITATIONS:
● Lose all Powers under red sun radiation
● X-Ray Vision cannot penetrate lead

VULNERABILITIES:
(All Loss Vulnerabilities affect Attributes, Powers, and Skills)
Rare Fatal and Loss:
Green Kryptonite: Range: 3
Rare Miscellaneous: (bizarre changes)
Red Kryptonite: Range: 3
Rare Miscellaneous Loss: (Permanent)
Gold Kryptonite: Range: 3
Magic Miscellaneous:
All Powers, Skills, and attributes against Mystical Powers or objects are at 4 APs
Miscellaneous Loss:
Gravity attacks subtract their RAPs from all of Phantom Zoner's

Abilities, but Abilities cannot be reduced to below 0 APs

EQUIPMENT:

SUPER UNIFORM

DEX:	0	STR:	0	BODY:	25
CHARGES:	NA				
COST:	991 HPs + $ 350M				

POWERS:
Skin Armor: 10

Unfortunately for Superman, there are criminals in the Phantom Zone who are much more than typical. Some of the better-known Phantom Zone villains' statistics and backgrounds are given below:

AZ-REL *Deceased*

DEX:	21	STR:	46	BODY:	34
INT:	6	WILL:	5	MIND:	7
INFL:	8	AURA:	4	SPIRIT:	3
INITIATIVE:	35	HERO POINTS:	65		

POWERS:
Directional Hearing: 10, Extended Hearing: 10, Flight: 45, Heat Vision: 30, Invulnerability: 45, Sealed Systems: 20, Solar Sustenance: 50, Super Breath: 20, Super Hearing: 10, Superspeed: 22, Systemic Antidote: 20, Telescopic Vision: 15, Thermal Vision: 15, X-Ray Vision: 20

SKILLS:
Gadgetry: 9, Scientist: 15, Thief: 7

LIMITATIONS:
● Lose all Powers under red sun radiation
● X-Ray Vision cannot penetrate lead

VULNERABILITIES:
(All Loss Vulnerabilities affect Attributes, Powers, and Skills)
Rare Fatal and Loss:
Green Kryptonite: Range: 3
Rare Miscellaneous: (bizarre changes)
Red Kryptonite: Range: 3
Rare Miscellaneous Loss: (Permanent)
Gold Kryptonite: Range: 3
Magic Miscellaneous:
All Abilities against Mystical Powers or objects are at 4 APs
Miscellaneous Loss:
Gravity attacks subtract their

RAPs from all of Phantom Zoner's Abilities, but Abilities cannot be reduced to below 0 APs

EQUIPMENT:

SUPER UNIFORM

DEX:	0	STR:	0	BODY:	25
CHARGES:	NA				
COST:	991 HPs + $ 350M				

POWERS:
Skin Armor: 10

NADIRA

DEX:	21	STR:	48	BODY:	36
INT:	5	WILL:	6	MIND:	6
INFL:	7	AURA:	3	SPIRIT:	3
INITIATIVE:	33	HERO POINTS:	65		

POWERS:
Directional Hearing: 10, Extended Hearing: 10, Flame Project: 25, Flight: 45, Heat Vision: 30, Invulnerability: 45, Sealed Systems: 20, Solar Sustenance: 50, Super Breath: 20, Super Hearing: 10, Superspeed: 22, Systemic Antidote: 20, Telescopic Vision: 15, Thermal Vision: 15, X-Ray Vision: 20

SKILLS:
Thief: 7, Vehicles: 4

LIMITATIONS:
● Lose all Powers under red sun radiation
● X-Ray Vision cannot penetrate lead

VULNERABILITIES:
(All Loss Vulnerabilities affect Attributes, Powers, and Skills)
Rare Fatal and Loss:
Green Kryptonite: Range: 3
Rare Miscellaneous: (bizarre changes)
Red Kryptonite: Range: 3
Rare Miscellaneous Loss: (permanent)
Gold Kryptonite: Range: 3
Magic Miscellaneous:
All Powers, Skills, and attributes against Mystical Powers or objects are at 4 APs
Miscellaneous Loss:
Gravity attacks subtract their RAPs from all of Phantom Zoner's Abilities, but Abilities cannot be reduced to below 0 APs.

EQUIPMENT:

SUPER UNIFORM

DEX: 0	STR: 0	BODY: 25
CHARGES: NA		
COST: 991 HPs + $ 350M		

POWERS:

Skin Armor: 10

Az-Rel and his partner Nadira were criminals from Bokos, the Kryptonian island of thieves. They were banished from the island due to their vast powers of destruction, but they were captured shortly after arriving at Kryptonopolis. The pair was sentenced to the Phantom Zone. Az-Rel and Nadira were killed during the mass escape, in which many of the Zone's inmates became corporeal and appeared on Earth.

FAORA HU-UL

DEX: 25	STR: 47	BODY: 37
INT: 9	WILL: 14	MIND: 12
INFL: 9	AURA: 8	SPIRIT: 5
INITIATIVE: 43 (52)	HERO POINTS: 175	

POWERS:
Directional Hearing: 10, Extended Hearing: 10, Flight: 45, Heat Vision: 30, Invulnerability: 45, Mental Blast: 32, Sealed Systems: 20, Solar Sustenance: 50, Super Breath: 20, Super Hearing: 10, Superspeed: 22, Systemic Antidote: 20, Telescopic Vision: 15, Thermal Vision: 15, X-Ray Vision: 20

SKILLS:
Acrobatics: 8, Charisma/Intimidation: 15, Gadgetry: 7, Martial Artist: 9

LIMITATIONS:
- Lose all Powers under red sun radiation
- X-Ray Vision cannot penetrate lead
- Catastrophic Irrational Attraction: Hatred of men

VULNERABILITIES:
(All Loss Vulnerabilities affect Attributes, Powers, and Skills)

Rare Fatal and Loss:
Green Kryptonite: Range: 3

Rare Miscellaneous:
(bizarre changes)
Red Kryptonite: Range: 3

Rare Miscellaneous Loss: (Permanent)
Gold Kryptonite: Range: 3

Magic Miscellaneous:
All Powers, Skills, and attributes against Mystical Powers or objects are at 4 APs

Miscellaneous Loss:
Gravity attacks subtract their RAPs from all of Phantom Zoner's Abilities, but Abilities cannot be reduced to below 0 APs

EQUIPMENT:

SUPER UNIFORM		
DEX: 0	STR: 0	BODY: 25
CHARGES: NA		
COST: 991 HPs + $ 350M		

POWERS:
Skin Armor: 10

SPECIAL: Due to Faora's special training in Horu-Kanu, when she attacks a Kryptonian (even a powered one), his/her Physical Attributes and any defensive powers are reduced to 4 APs. Damage to the victim's BODY is treated as per damage under the Magic Vulnerability (see *Superman and Magic*).

In the grasslands of Alezer, Krypton's police captured Faora after 23 men had been methodically tortured to death at her hands. Her mastery of the deadly art of Horu-Kanu was so complete that the police were forced to shoot her down from the air.

Perhaps the only true psychopath sentenced to the Zone, Faora's hatred of men, her martial arts, her ruthlessness, and her cunning all combine to make her perhaps *the* most dangerous of all the Phantom Zone inmates. It is known that she has survived to the 30th Century.

GENERAL DRU-ZOD		
DEX: 25	STR: 48	BODY: 38
INT: 12	WILL: 20	MIND: 14
INFL: 10	AURA: 6	SPIRIT: 4
INITIATIVE: 47	HERO POINTS: 180	

POWERS:
Directional Hearing: 10, Extended Hearing: 10, Flight: 45, Heat Vision: 30, Invulnerability: 45, Sealed Systems: 20, Solar Sustenance: 50, Super Breath: 20, Super Hearing: 10, Superspeed: 22, Systemic Antidote: 20, Telescopic Vision: 15, Thermal Vision: 15, X-Ray Vision: 20

SKILLS:
Charisma: 17, Gadgetry: 9, Military Science: 10, Spy: 8, Vehicles: 7, Weaponry: 12

LIMITATIONS:
• Lose all Powers under red sun radiation
• X-Ray Vision cannot penetrate lead

VULNERABILITIES:
(All Loss Vulnerabilities affect Attributes, Powers, and Skills)

Rare Fatal and Loss:
Green Kryptonite: Range: 3

Rare Miscellaneous: (bizarre changes:
Red Kryptonite: Range: 3

Rare Miscellaneous Loss: (permanent)
Gold Kryptonite: Range: 3

Magic Miscellaneous:
All Abilities against Mystical Powers or objects are at 4 APs

Miscellaneous Loss:
Gravity attacks subtract their RAPs from all of Phantom Zoner's Abilities, but Abilities cannot be reduced to below 0 APs

EQUIPMENT:

SUPER UNIFORM		
DEX: 0	STR: 0	BODY: 25
CHARGES: NA		
COST: 991 HPs + $ 350M		

POWERS:
Skin Armor: 10

Dru-Zod, general of Krypton's army, used his genius to construct non-organic duplicates of himself. The duplicates were perfect soldiers willing to sacrifice their lives for their leader. Zod tried to use them to capture Fort Rozz, Krypton's major defense center, as the first step in his conquest of Krypton and, eventually, the universe.

He underestimated Krypton's resolve against him and was defeated, tried, and sent to the Zone. His military training and technical expertise have more than once made life difficult for Superman. It is known he has survived to the 30th Century.

JAX-UR		
DEX: 21	STR: 47	BODY: 36
INT: 9	WILL: 8	MIND: 11
INFL: 6	AURA: 3	SPIRIT: 4
INITIATIVE: 36	HERO POINTS: 80	

POWERS:
Directional Hearing: 10, Extended Hearing: 10, Flight: 45, Heat Vision: 30, Invulnerability: 45, Sealed Systems: 20, Solar Sustenance: 50, Super Breath: 20, Super Hearing: 10, Superspeed: 22, Systemic Antidote: 20, Telescopic Vision: 15, Thermal Vision: 15, X-Ray Vision: 20

SKILLS:
Gadgetry: 13, Scholar (Astrophysics): 12, Scientist: 17

LIMITATIONS:
• Loses all Powers under red sun radiation
• X-Ray Vision cannot penetrate lead

VULNERABILITIES:
(All Loss Vulnerabilities affect Attributes, Powers, and Skills)

Rare Fatal and Loss:
Green Kryptonite: Range: 3

Rare Miscellaneous: (bizarre changes)
Red Kryptonite: Range: 3

Rare Miscellaneous Loss: (permanent)
Gold Kryptonite: Range: 3

Magic Miscellaneous:
all Powers, Skills, and attributes against Mystical Powers or objects are at 4 APs

Miscellaneous Loss:
Gravity attacks subtract their RAPs from all of Phantom Zoner's Abilities, but Abilities cannot be reduced to below 0 APs

EQUIPMENT:

SUPER UNIFORM		
DEX: 0	STR: 0	BODY: 25
CHARGES: NA		
COST: 991 HPs + $ 350M		

POWERS:
Skin Armor: 10

A renegade scientist and former co-worker of Jor-El, Jax-Ur had the dubious honor of being the first Phantom Zone inmate. He created a nuclear missile which he planned to demonstrate by destroying a meteor. However, the guidance system failed and the rocket exploded, destroying Krypton's colonized moon, Wegthor. This occurrence led to the Science Council's decision to ban further space experiments, thus forcing Jor-El to conduct his own rocket experiments in secret.

JER-EM *Deceased*		
DEX: 19	STR: 44	BODY: 34
INT: 5	WILL: 16	MIND: 9
INFL: 10	AURA: 9	SPIRIT: 8
INITIATIVE: 34	HERO POINTS: 55	

POWERS:

Directional Hearing: 10, Extended Hearing: 10, Flight: 45, Heat Vision: 30, Invulnerability: 45, Sealed Systems: 20, Solar Sustenance: 50, Super Breath: 20, Super Hearing: 10, Superspeed: 22, Systemic Antidote: 20, Telescopic Vision: 15, Thermal Vision: 15, X-Ray Vision: 20

SKILLS:

Charisma: 7, Scholar/Academic Study (Raoism): 6

LIMITATIONS:

● Loses all Powers under red sun radiation

● X-Ray Vision cannot penetrate lead

VULNERABILITIES:

(All Loss Vulnerabilities affect Attributes, Powers, and Skills)

Rare Fatal and Loss:
Green Kryptonite: Range: 3

Rare Miscellaneous:
(bizarre changes)
Red Kryptonite: Range: 3

Rare Miscellaneous Loss:
(Permanent)
Gold Kryptonite: Range: 3

Magic Miscellaneous:
All Powers, Skills, and attributes against Mystical Powers or objects are at 4 APs

Miscellaneous Loss:
Gravity attacks subtract their RAPs from all of Phantom Zoner's Abilities, but Abilities cannot be reduced to below 0 APs

EQUIPMENT:

```
SUPER UNIFORM
DEX:   0  STR:   0  BODY: 25
CHARGES: NA
COST:  991 HPs+$ 350M
```

POWERS:
Skin Armor: 10

Jer-Em was known as the "mad prophet" of Argo City. He inadvertently destroyed the city and was Argo's last exile to the Zone. When the mass escape from the Zone took place, Jer-Em was exposed to Kryptonite and died.

```
KRU-EL
DEX:  20  STR:  47  BODY: 38
INT:  10  WILL:  9  MIND: 11
INFL:  8  AURA:  4  SPIRIT: 3
INITIATIVE: 38  HERO POINTS: 80
```

POWERS:
Directional Hearing: 10, Extended Hearing: 10, Flight: 45, Heat Vision: 30, Invulnerability: 45, Sealed Systems: 20, Solar Sustenance: 50, Super Breath: 20, Super Hearing: 10, Superspeed: 22, Systemic Antidote: 20, Telescopic Vision: 15, Thermal Vision: 15, X-Ray Vision: 20

SKILLS:
Gadgetry: 11, Scientist: 16, Weaponry: 7

LIMITATIONS:
• Loses all Powers under red sun radiation
• X-Ray Vision cannot penetrate lead

VULNERABILITIES:
(All Loss Vulnerabilities affect Attributes, Powers, and Skills)
Rare Fatal and Loss:
Green Kryptonite: Range: 3
Rare Miscellaneous:
(bizarre changes)
Red Kryptonite: Range: 3

Rare Miscellaneous Loss:
(permanent)
Gold Kryptonite: Range: 3
Magic Miscellaneous:
All Powers, Skills, and attributes against Mystical Powers or objects are at 4 APs
Miscellaneous Loss:
Gravity attacks subtract their RAPs from all of Phantom Zoner's Abilities, but Abilities cannot be reduced to below 0 APs

EQUIPMENT:

```
SUPER UNIFORM
DEX:   0  STR:   0  BODY: 25
CHARGES: NA
COST:  991 HPs+$ 350M
```

POWERS:
Skin Armor: 10

The mind of Kru-El is almost as brilliant as that of his cousin, Jor-El. However, Kru-El's mind is evil and twisted. He built a cache of forbidden weapons of terrible destructive potential. Shot down by Jor-El, Kru-El was the next to the last Zone inmate from Krypton, followed only by the innocent Quex-Ul.

```
VA-KOX
DEX:  21  STR:  48  BODY: 38
INT:  10  WILL:  8  MIND: 10
INFL:  6  AURA:  3  SPIRIT: 4
INITIATIVE: 37  HERO POINTS: 85
```

POWERS:
Directional Hearing: 10, Extended Hearing: 10, Flight: 45, Heat Vision: 30, Invulnerability: 45, Sealed Systems: 20, Solar Sustenance: 50, Super Breath: 20, Super Hearing: 10, Superspeed: 22, Systemic Antidote: 20, Telescopic Vision: 15, Thermal Vision: 15, X-Ray Vision: 20

SKILLS:
Gadgetry: 8, Scholar/Academic Study (Biology): 9, Scientist: 12

LIMITATIONS:
• Lose all Powers under red sun radiation
• X-Ray Vision cannot penetrate lead

VULNERABILITIES:
(All Loss Vulnerabilities affect Attributes, Powers, and Skills)
Rare Fatal and Loss:
Green Kryptonite: Range: 3
Rare Miscellaneous:
(bizarre changes)
Red Kryptonite: Range: 3
Rare Miscellaneous Loss:
(permanent)
Gold Kryptonite: Range: 3
Magic Miscellaneous:
All Powers, Skills, and attributes against Mystical Powers or objects are at 4 APs
Miscellaneous Loss:
Gravity attacks subtract their RAPs from all Abilities, but Abilities cannot be reduced to below 0 APs

EQUIPMENT:

```
SUPER UNIFORM
DEX:   0  STR:   0  BODY: 25
CHARGES: NA
COST:  991 HPs+$ 350M
```

POWERS:
Skin Armor: 10

Professor Va-Kox's experiments in altering the evolution of marine life in Krypton's Great Lake produced hideous monsters. His experiments also poisoned the water potentially for 50 of Krypton's sun-cycles. Va-Kox was sentenced to the Zone for that period of time. However, Krypton exploded before his sentence was over. Va-Kox lived on to be one of the Zone's greatest schemers.

```
NAM-EK
DEX:  20  STR:  48  BODY: 50
INT:   8  WILL:  7  MIND: 12
INFL:  7  AURA:  4  SPIRIT: 5
INITIATIVE: 35  HERO POINTS: 160
```

POWERS:
Directional Hearing: 10, Extended Hearing: 10, Flight: 45, Heat Vision: 30, Invulnerability: 45, Regeneration: 20, Sealed Systems: 20, Solar Sustenance: 50, Super Breath: 20, Super

Hearing: 10, Superspeed: 22, Systemic Antidote: 20, Telescopic Vision: 15, Thermal Vision: 15, Transfer (Regeneration only): 20, X-Ray Vision: 20

SKILLS:
Medicine: 8, Scientist: 12

LIMITATIONS:
● Only Invulnerability, Regeneration, and Transfer will function under red sun radiation.
● X-Ray Vision can't penetrate lead.

VULNERABILITIES:
Magic Miscellaneous:
All Powers, Skills, and attributes against Mystical Powers or objects are at 4 APs

Miscellaneous Loss:
Gravity attacks subtract their RAPs from all Abilities, but Abilities cannot be reduced to below 0 APs

EQUIPMENT:

SUPER UNIFORM		
DEX: 0	STR: 0	BODY: 25
CHARGES: NA		
COST: 991 HPs + $ 350M		

POWERS:
Skin Armor: 10

Five hundred years before the fall of Krypton, the hunter Nam-Ek illegally slew a Rondor, a creature whose horn radiated a natural healing ray which cured all sickness and mended all injury. From the Rondor's horn, Nam-Ek distilled an elixir that would prevent death.

Nam-Ek paid a horrible price for immortality: he was mutated into a human Rondor, ugly and foul-smelling. He served a term of literally "life" imprisonment, but even the explosion of Krypton could not end his life.

It should be noted that despite some contradictory reports, Nam-Ek was not banished to the Phantom Zone from Krypton. Drifting through space, Nam-Ek eventually came to Earth, where he battled Superman. He was ultimately defeated and banished to the Zone. However, he is one of the few inmates who does not bear Superman animosity; his current body and immortality comprise a greater prison than anything else existing.

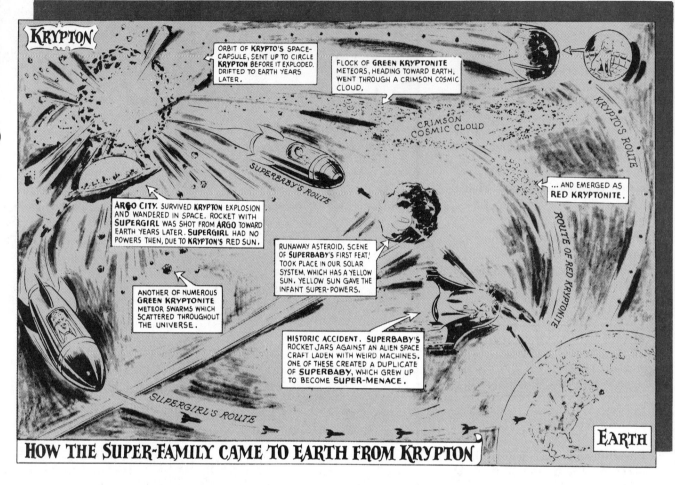

HOW THE SUPER-FAMILY CAME TO EARTH FROM KRYPTON

Unlike many planets, Krypton was not created by the gravitational condensation of gasses around a sun. It was formed by a race of gaseous beings called the Sun-Thrivers. The Sun-Thrivers created a giant red sun in which to dwell, only to discover it to be unstable. So they created planets from a portion of the solar matter to stabilize the star; one of these planets was a solid "giant" world which became known as Krypton.

Civilization on Krypton, which started 10,000 Kryptonian years ago, evolved slowly. Several barbarian tribes on the main continent of Urrika were united by Erok, who had imbibed a potion endowing him with great strength. Erok hoped to subdue the rival tribes and unite them.

Erok ruled the tribes well, becoming a great civilizer and lawgiver. He formed Erok City, which became known as Erokul and survived up to the planet's destruction. Erok outlawed the practices of cannibalism and human sacrifice. He also started the practice of using family names. He adapted the surname of El (meaning "star") and is the first documented ancestor of Superman.

Civilization grew. The descendants of Erok-El made many scientific discoveries, such as the telescope and the compass.

The religions worshiped many gods in a vaguely polytheistic system. Jaf-El, a prophet of the sun-god Rao, preached the worship of his deity alone and made several accurate predictions. One of his visions foretold a great flood. When the waters rose, many people were saved by the huge winged creatures, "Tanthuo Flez," which were summoned by Jaf's brother Tio-El. Taking their rescue to be a sign from Rao, the people adopted him as the one true god.

The floods signaled the end of the Urrikan Empire and the people settled into villages. The villages eventually evolved into city-states. During this time an alien race invaded Krypton, but the Kryptonians eventually threw off the yoke of oppression, using the invaders' own weapons against them.

Approximately 150 years before Krypton's destruction, the last great war ended. A world federation was formed, with Kandor as its capital. All of the natives were united except for the black-skinned people of the island Valthio and the thieves of the criminal empire of Bokos.

Science had progressed apace over the centuries, aided by the alien technology which the Kryptonians were able to analyze and duplicate. Space travel as a science was never really developed, however, as the population was relatively small and there was much land to be explored. Early attempts were thwarted by the existence of a space-being called Zazura who fed on the death-throes of sentient life. Although the menace of Zazura was thwarted when the Kryptonians seeded their atmosphere with her one weakness, a red ore from Krypton's firefalls, the few astronauts who flew to the stars never returned.

After the wars, it was decided that Krypton, as the united peoples now called their nation, would be ruled by a technocracy. During the last 150 years, Kryptonian knowledge seemed to stagnate, with no new challenges. When one of the planet's leading scientists, Jor-El, came to the Science Council and announced his theory about Krypton's impending doom, they rejected his findings. The Council was confident that, since Krypton had stood for millions of years, it would continue for many more.

Jor-El tried to push through the development of a space program, but it was halted when his assistant Jax-Ur destroyed one of Krypton's two moons, killing thousands of colonists. Jor-El also attempted to create a fleet of space arks, aided by his supporters in Kandor. Unfortunately, the space-villain Brainiac miniaturized and stole that city before the fleet's construction was completed.

Stripped of resources by Kandor's theft, Jor-El struggled desperately to construct a rocket that could take his family to safety in the weeks remaining before Krypton's imminent destruction. Unfortunately, he only succeeded in building a rocket large enough for his wife and son. His wife chose to remain behind with her husband, but he sent his son Kal-El out just in time.

There were three main groups of Kryptonian survivors. Argo City, covered by a weatherproof dome, was thrown off into space and survived for many years. The bottle city of Kandor was later recovered from Brainiac, and the natives were eventually returned to their normal size and went to live on the planet Rokyn. There are also a number of Kryptonians who are still prisoners in the Phantom Zone.

KRYPTONESE GLOSSARY

Following is a short list of Kryptonese words and terms. They have been translated as closely as possible from the original, but some spellings are approximations due to the fact that the Kryptonese alphabet possesses 118 letters, each representing a particular sound.

As the letter 'S' is added to a noun in English to make it a plural, so is the letter 'O' in Kryptonese.

AMPAR: Commander, captain, or chief officer.

AMZET: One year, which consisted of 73 weeks of six days each.

BETHGAR: A ruler; roughly equivalent to our King or Emperor.

BYTHGAR: The feminine form of Bethgar; equivalent to Queen or Empress.

DENDARO: Plural of Dendar, a Kryptonian "minute," consisting of 100 *Thribo*, the equivalent of Earth seconds.

DROTHO: Plural of Droth, a type of large sea-bird that fed chiefly on *Silten*.

DRYGUR: A word meaning "leader;" roughly equivalent to our "president."

DRYGUR-MOLIOM: The leader of the Science Council.

EL: An ancient Kryptonese word meaning "star".

FANFF: Six days, making a Kryptonian "week."

GRAHU: An artificial material, somewhat like plastic, but much stronger, used for building on Krypton.

HATUAR: A word meaning a certain asbestos-like substance, named for its creator, Hatu-El.

HIAZ: A liquid measure used in ancient Krypton. It was somewhere between one pint and one-half liter.

LORAXO: Plural of Lorax, a period of 73 days, making a Kryptonian month. Six of these months made an *Amzet*, or year.

MOLIOM: Any member of the Science Council.

OLIPHENT: A type of large animal domesticated and used as a beast of burden. Despite the similarity to our word "elephant," there was little resemblance to this Earth creature except that both are large. The Oliphent was not even a mammal, but a warm-blooded egg-laying creature.

PRYLIGU: A large sea-monster of Krypton.

SILTEN: A type of edible algae or seaweed.

TANTHO: Plural of Tanth, a term of respect for a man, roughly equivalent to our Sir or Gentleman.

TANTHUO FLEZ: From the same root as *Tanth*, Tanthu (the singular) cannot be exactly translated into English, as there is no equivalent word. It indicates a non-human creature accorded great respect. Combined with Flez, meaning "able to fly," the term is used for the amazing beings which saved many Kryptonians from a great deluge of the distant past.

THRIB: A very short period of time, equivalent to an Earth second.

TWELLIAN: A succculent fruit native to Krypton. Its flavor is unlike that of any Earth fruit, but it is quite delicious.

TYNTHO: Plural of Tynth, the feminine of Tanth. It means, roughly, Lady or Madame.

WOLU: A Kryptonian "hour," consisting of 100 *Dendaro*.

YAGRUM: A particularly dangerous, but rare, monster once found on Krypton.

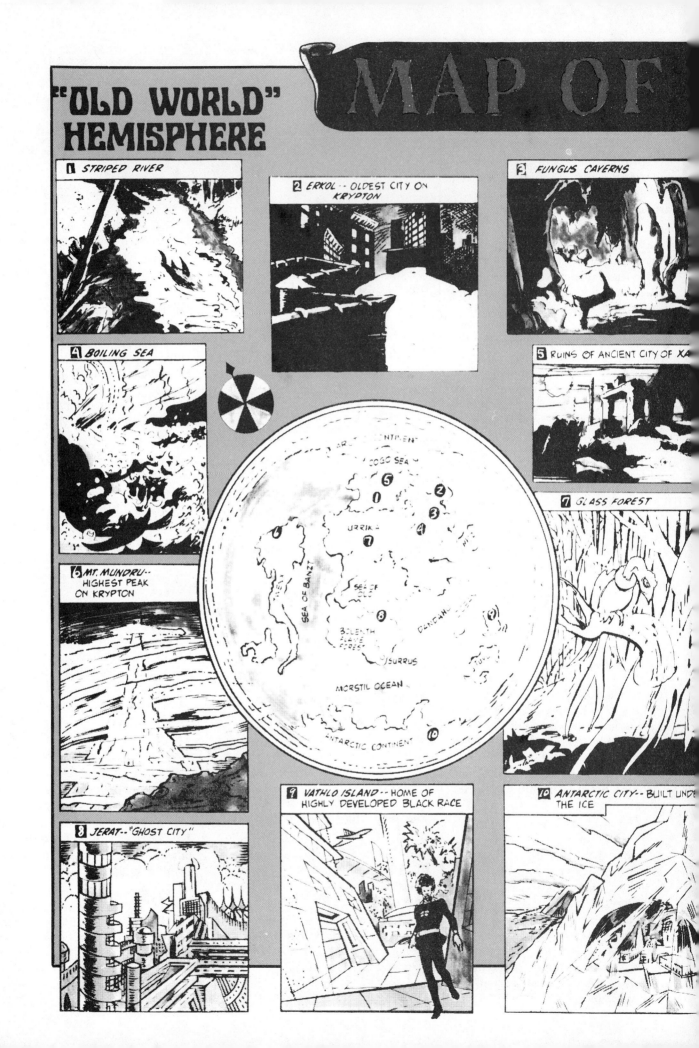

RYPTON
"NEW WORLD" HEMISPHERE

1 KANDOR--CAPITAL OF KRYPTON UNTIL IT WAS STOLEN BY BRAINIAC

2 KRYPTONOPOLIS-- SUPERMAN'S BIRTH- PLACE; KRYPTON'S 2ND CAPITAL

3 UNDERSEA PALACE

4 FORT ROZZ--MAIN DEFENSE CENTER

5 ATOMIC TOWN

6 JEWEL MOUNTAINS

5 LOST VALLEY OF JURU-- UNEXPLORED (NO PICTURES AVAILABLE)

8 GOLD VOLCANO

7 RAINBOW CANYON

10 SCARLET JUNGLE

9 FIRE FALLS

12 ARGO CITY-- SUPERGIRL'S BIRTHPLACE

13 BOKOS-- INDEPENDENT ISLAND OF THIEVES

14 MAGNETIC MOUNTAIN

11 METEOR VALLEY

KRYPTONITE

The material which has come to be known as "Kryptonite" is actually debris from the planet Krypton. The high pressures at the unstable core, combined with the massive levels of radiation, caused all of Krypton's substance to transform into a new element.

Kryptonite has a high atomic weight, but, unlike most other radioactive elements, it is reasonably stable. Ironically, it is the only substance from Krypton which does not become indestructible under a yellow sun. It is highly friction-resistant, which is why there are so many pieces of considerable size on Earth.

However, no *natural* phenomena can account for the large quantities of Kryptonite that have been found on Earth. The explanation for this lies in the fact the space-warp which Kal-El's rocket was launched through to reach Earth has remained partially open all of these years. As a result, a great deal of Krypton's substance has passed through this warp and crashed to Earth.

Like most radioactive elements, Kryptonite eventually decays into a more stable substance which, for Kryptonite, is iron. This process can take centuries. However, a nuclear experiment once triggered off a chain

reaction which transformed all of the Kryptonite on Earth into iron; more has since landed.

Using samples of Kryptonite that have crashed to Earth, several criminal scientists, including Lex Luthor, have devised a means of synthesizing Green Kryptonite. The process is prohibitively expensive, but its use as a weapon against Superman usually makes such an investment worthwhile for those of less than honest intent. Fortunately for Superman, Green Kryptonite is apparently the only isotope of Kryptonite capable of artificial duplication.

Although Kryptonite is most effective through simple exposure, it can also be used as a power source. Metallo uses Kryptonite to power his cyborg body, but he has sought a number of alternate power sources due to the relative scarcity of Kryptonite. Lex Luthor, among others, has used both real and artificial Green Kryptonite to power a wide variety of weapons for use against the Man of Tomorrow.

When any villain uses a Green Kryptonite-powered weapon to attack Superman, Superman receives a -4 Column Shift to his OV/RV. (Only Green Kryptonite yields enough energy to be used as a power source.) Even Green Kryptonite-powered machines making Mental or Mystical attacks receive this 4-column bonus against Superman.

Kryptonite's unique radiations almost always affect Kryptonians only. Natives of other Krypton-like planets, such as Karb-Brak and Mon-El, appear to be indifferent to Kryptonite. Kryptonite can even help to neutralize the effects of lead poisoning in Daxamites. Brainiac 5, a member of the Legion of Super-Heroes, has used Kryptonite to formulate a cure for Mon-El, who was trapped in the Phantom Zone until the 30th Century due to lead poisoning.

For a number of different reasons, various isotopes of Kryptonite have come into existence over the years. Some are unique in that they can affect non-Kryptonians, and several are artificial isotopes created through laboratory accidents. Listed here are the only known isotopes to date:

GREEN KRYPTONITE neutralizes powers in Kryptonians and causes blood poisoning, resulting in death in 7-9 APs (or, more precisely, in 128 to 512 phases). It has no effect on non-powered Kryptonians.

ANTI-KRYPTONITE is also green in color. It causes blood poisoning in non-powered Kryptonians, resulting in death in 7-9 APs. The chunk of Krypton that Argo City rested upon was of this substance.

X-KRYPTONITE, the third green-colored isotope, was accidentally created by Supergirl during an experiment. It endows humans with powers similar to those of Kryptonians. The duration of these powers is initially temporary, but can be made permanent.

SLOW-KRYPTONITE, the final of the four green-colored isotopes, is one of the few types of Kryptonite that affects normal human beings. It causes loss of BODY APs in humans just as it does in Kryptonians. It was created by an Earth scientist in an unrepeatable experiment, and Metallo gained access to it. He abandoned it after a battle with Batman.

RED KRYPTONITE is Green Kryptonite which has passed through a strange red gas cloud and is drastically altered. Each piece of Red Kryptonite can cause a different bizarre effect on a Kryptonian, and each piece will have the same effect on any Kryptonian. One piece of Red Kryptonite can only affect an individual Kryptonian once. The effect lasts for a period of 24-48 hours.

The Gamemaster will have to determine the effects of any given piece of Red Kryptonite. Some of the effects seen in the past have been: turning Superman into: a dragon, a non-powered giant, a midget, an ant-headed humanoid, a lunatic, and an amnesiac; causing him to grow incredibly long hair and beard; rendering him powerless; causing him to lose his Invulnerability along the left side of his body; splitting him into an evil Superman and a good Clark Kent; and rendering him unable to speak or write anything but Kryptonese.

WHITE KRYPTONITE affects non-Kryptonian life. It will kill any plant life within 3 APs.

BLUE KRYPTONITE is another artificial creation which will only affect Bizarros. It has the same effect on Bizarros as Green Kryptonite has on Kryptonians. This isotope was created by Superman when he used the Bizarro Duplicator Ray on a piece of Green Kryptonite. The Man of Steel once used Blue Kryptonite to repel an invasion of Earth by the Bizarro Superman.

GOLD KRYPTONITE is debris from the Gold Volcano on Krypton. It is probably the rarest of all Kryptonite isotopes, and its effects are the most drastic of all. A Kryptonian exposed to Gold Kryptonite will lose his or her powers, or any possibility of ever having powers (even through the use of X-Kryptonite or other artificial means). Even a moment's exposure is sufficient to strip a Kryptonian of his/her powers.

Apparently, Superman has never been exposed to this substance, nor have Supergirl, Krypto, or any of the Phantom Zoners. The wrongly convicted Zoner Quex-Ul was exposed to Gold Kryptonite when he attempted to take revenge on Superman after being released at the end of his sentence (see *The Phantom Zone* for additional details).

JEWEL KRYPTONITE is also very rare. It was created by the Phantom Zone villain Jax-Ur, who travelled back in time on one occasion to the Jewel Mountains on Krypton. There, he prepared special crystals which were transformed into Jewel Kryptonite when Krypton exploded.

Jewel Kryptonite is not Kryptonite in the accepted sense of the word, in that it does not give off debilitating radiation and is probably not even a radioactive element. It does allow the Phantom Zoners to use their mental forces to alter and affect things outside the Zone.

A Character in the Phantom Zone can focus his mental energies through a piece of Jewel Kryptonite by making a roll with the Character's INT/MIND as the AV/EV and 4/4 as the OV/RV. The RAPs can be used as APs of Control, Hypnotism, Illusion, Mental Blast, or Mind Blast; the Character does not have to have these Powers already. These can be directed at anyone within 20 APs of the Jewel Kryptonite, and a new roll must be made once per day to determine if the available APs change. Multiple Zoners can attempt to use the Jewel Kryptonite to generate APs while using the normal bonuses for a Multi-Attack.

Although the Zoners can Mental or Mind Blast opponents with the Jewel Kryptonite (and will, as a last resort), they prefer to use the substance to gain some more subtle advantage, resulting in their escape, the death of Superman, or some other objective.

SUPERMAN'S EQUIPMENT

One would think that Superman, with all his vast powers, would hardly need anything else. In fact, the Man of Tomorrow uses a variety of equipment from time to time. Some of the more memorable items are listed below:

SUPER UNIFORM

DEX:	0	STR:	0	BODY:	25
CHARGES:	NA				
COST:	991 HPs + $ 350M				

POWERS:
Skin Armor: 10

Superman's costume was created for him by Ma Kent. When young Clark first began to display his powers as a baby, the Kents concluded that their clothing bill was going to go up at a horrendous rate if something wasn't done about the wear and tear that Clark's antics were causing.

One day, a freak fire occurred in the Kents' attic when a lightning bolt struck the house. Young Clark put out the fire with his Super Breath.

During the aftermath of the fire, Ma and Pa Kent discovered a discarded set of blankets from the rocket in which they had found their adopted son. They noticed that the red, yellow, and blue material was completely unscathed. Seeing the blankets as a possible solution for their son's clothing needs, the couple put the blankets

through extensive tests until they were satisfied that the material was the closest thing to indestructible that they would ever find.

Martha managed to unravel the blankets, with a little help from Clark's Heat Vision. She knitted a special playsuit for him to wear.

Later, when Clark first decided to appear as Superboy, he felt that he needed a special costume. He helped his mother unravel his baby suit so that she could make him a new, larger uniform. He made the seat-belt that had strapped him into the rocket into a belt for his costume, and created boots from the upholstery in the rocket's compartment. He also used the upholstery material to create a stylized "S" to wear upon his chest.

Along with the Skin Armor Power, the Super Uniform also has several other uses not so readily apparent. Superman can wrap an individual (or up to 5 APs of volume) within his cape, providing that Character or item with protection from heat friction while that Character or item is being carried at high Flight speeds. It will also contain enough air and is well enough insulated to provide whatever is wrapped within the equivalent of 9 APs of Sealed Systems. This cannot be pushed, however.

The Super Uniform is also very stretchable, out to 9 APs. Superman

has often used his cape as a net (or anything else necessary). As Superman has grown over the years, the costume has also stretched to fit him. And can still be compressed into a small bundle and concealed.

Fortunately for Superman, the Super Uniform has provided him with superior protection on a number of occasions when he has lost his powers. Unfortunately, it also has been stolen from him several times. Superman has a selection of similar uniforms, but they are made of relatively weak material (with no Skin Armor).

As with any Kryptonian material, Superman's uniform will lose all of its properties when exposed to red sun radiation. It becomes nothing more than ordinary cloth and metal under such circumstances.

SUBSTITUTE UNIFORM

DEX:	0	STR:	0	BODY:	6
CHARGES:	NA				
COST:	48 HPs + $ 600				

GLASSES

DEX: 0	STR:	0	BODY:	25/2*	
CHARGES:	NA				
COST:	888 HPs + $ 270M				

* BODY of Lenses/Frames

When creating his "Clark Kent" disguise after becoming Superboy, Clark felt that a pair of glasses would complete his timid appearance. Unfortunately, he frequently needed to use his Heat Vision (which is normally invisible to human eyes) without being seen. Clark discovered that the standard glass lenses would simply melt in the frames.

Clark sought a solution to this problem. He discovered that several fairly round pieces had broken off from the windshield of his rocket when it landed on Earth. So he put two suitable pieces of this substance into a pair of frames that would conceal the jagged edges. The lenses, as durable as any Kryptonian material, were more than adequate to withstand the incredible temperatures of his Heat Vision.

The lenses are essentially clear pieces of glass; this has been noticed by several individuals who merely think it a near-normal prescription.

Superman has since had several pairs fabricated for him by Kandorian glass smiths. These pairs are far less crude than his originals.

SUPERBOY ROBOTS

DEX:	15	STR:	40	BODY:	35
INT:	11	WILL:	2	MIND:	3
INFL:	0	AURA:	0	SPIRIT:	0
INITIATIVE:	26	HERO POINTS:	0		
CHARGES:	65				
COST:	9594 HPs + $ 1.7T				

POWERS:(* linked)
Directional Hearing*: 11, Extended Hearing*: 11, Flight*: 15, Heat Vision*: 11, Microscopic Vision*: 11, Recall: 16, Sealed Systems: 16, Super Breath: 16, Super Hearing: 11, Superspeed*: 15, Systemic Antidote: 16, Telescopic Vision*: 11, Thermal Vision*: 11, X-Ray Vision*: 11

SKILLS:
Artist/Actor: 4

SUPERMAN ROBOTS

DEX:	20	STR:	45	BODY:	40
INT:	15	WILL:	4	MIND:	5
INFL:	0	AURA:	0	SPIRIT:	0
INITIATIVE:	35	HERO POINTS:	0		
CHARGES:	67				
COST:	14,615 HPs + $10.45T				

POWERS:
Directional Hearing*: 15, Extended Hearing*: 15, Flight*: 20, Heat Vision*: 15, Microscopic Vision*: 15, Recall: 20, Sealed Systems: 20, Super Breath: 20, Super Hearing*: 15, Superspeed*: 20, Systemic Antidote: 20, Telescopic Vision*: 15, Thermal Vision*: 15, X-Ray Vision*: 15

SKILLS:
Artist/Actor: 10

LIMITATIONS:
• Artist/Actor Skill only allows the robot to pass as the person it is made to look like.
• X-Ray Vision can't penetrate lead.

MOTIVATION: NA
WEALTH: NA
JOB: Superman (or Superboy)/Clark Kent stand-in
RACE: Artificial Life (robotic android)

The Superman robots (and their predecessors, the Superboy models) may be one of the Man of Tomorrow's most ingenious creations.

Clark first created the robots when he discovered that not even a Superboy could always be in two or more places at once. The first models were relatively crude mechanical duplicates, although Clark's skill in creating them steadily progressed. He had one major advantage over other boys who tinkered in their spare time. With his Superspeed, Clark could compress 24 APs of building time into 1 AP.

Clark kept as many as six robots on hand at any given time; they were stored in the Kents' basement in Smallville. Clark also had several models of "Clark Kent" robots but rarely used them, as they could not pass close scrutiny. Superboy would sometimes have one of the Clark Kent robots perform some feat while he was in the presence of Lana Lang or someone else in order to convince his friends that Clark and Superboy were two different individuals.

When Clark moved away to Metropolis, he scrapped the Superboy robots almost completely, keeping only one or two for mementos. As he grew older, he designed Superman robots of superior quality, using knowledge of robotics which he gained from studying the robots of criminal geniuses such as Lex Luthor. Because of the cramped quarters in his Metropolis apartment, Superman kept only one or two robots there (in a hidden closet). He kept many others at the Fortress of Solitude. He also maintained a hidden cache of robots at the Daily Planet, but ended this practice when it was discovered and his secret identity was almost revealed by Lois.

Superman's skill in robotics and artificial intelligence developed to the point that he could design lookalikes capable of withstanding all but the closest scrutiny. Although he rarely did so, he could leave for several hours on a mission as Superman and have a Clark Kent robot take Lois Lane out to dinner.

Superman's experiments in artificial intelligence have sometimes gone awry. On at least one occasion he created a robot that duplicated his engrams (memory building-blocks) so exactly that the robot believed that it was Superman. Several alien criminals took advantage of the robot's self-awareness in a plot to destroy Superman. The plan was foiled when the robot sacrificed its "life" for the Man of Steel. If another such robot was to be created, it would have INT: 15, WILL: 14, MIND: 12, Initiative: 30.

In recent years, the steadily increasing pollution level on Earth has caused the robots to seriously malfunction whenever they use their powers. Superman still uses them to cover for him as Clark Kent, but they are rarely seen otherwise.

SUPERMOBILE

DEX:	24	STR:	48	BODY:	45
CHARGES:	81				
COST:	21,295 HPs + $ 36.4T				

POWERS:
Flight: 45, Sealed Systems: 20

Special Capabilities: provides insulation against Kryptonite and red sun radiation. Seats two.

The Supermobile is a special vehicle. Superman has designed it for use in sustained battles in which he has a chance of being exposed to red sun radiation or Kryptonite.

Crafted from "Supermanium," an alloy of Superman's own design and harder than almost any other substance in the known universe, the Supermobile is essentially a "waldo" which allows Superman to use all of his powers. The Supermobile has a pair of mechanical arms to allow him to direct his strength and a series of projectors to allow him to use his various vision powers from inside the craft without any impairment. However, he cannot use Heat Vision, Invulnerability, Solar Sustenance, Super Breath, Superspeed, Super Ventriloquism, or Systemic Antidote on an object outside the Supermobile while he is inside.

Superman first used the craft when the Earth was being swept by a band of red sun radiation and the one-man Justice League, Amazo, was on a rampage. The Man of Steel has used it sporadically since, as the situation requires it, but he seems to feel that it is somewhat awkward and slows him down. In most situations, such as when he flew to Lexor to battle Lex Luthor just before that planet blew up, he will find other ways to avoid losing his powers.

PHANTOM ZONE PROJECTOR		
DEX: 0	STR: 0	BODY: 25
CHARGES: NA		
COST: 2225 HPs + $ 750M		

POWERS:
Dispersal: 25, Warp: 25

The Zone Projector was the creation of Jor-El of Krypton. He originally discovered the principle while trying to find a way of evacuating Krypton before its destruction. Although it was of no use in that capacity, Jor-El presented it to the Science Council as a means of imprisonment. It was accepted, and several Kryptonian criminals were sentenced to the Zone before Krypton's destruction.

The Science Council eventually declared that the Projector be launched into space along with a cache of forbidden weapons. The capsule containing the technological goodies eventually drifted through the warp that Jor-El's experimental rocket had created between Krypton's system and Earth; it was later discovered by Superboy.

With his high intelligence, the Boy

of Steel was quick to divine its capabilities. In the years since, he has used it to place other Kryptonian criminals in the Zone and release those whose sentences were up. The Bottle City of Kandor had a duplicate Zone Projector made, which they used for their own criminals.

The Projector is a small (3 AP) searchlight-like device. It is not easily carried by a normal man. Although it usually rests in the Fortress of Solitude, Superman has often used it as a weapon to capture some Kryptonian unawares.

It is known that at least one Projector has survived to the 30th Century, where it is a major exhibit in the Superman Museum in Metropolis. It was used by the Legion of Super-Heroes to recover their comrade Mon-El from the Zone after he suffered from a relapse of his lead poisoning.

ZONE-A-PHONE		
DEX: 0	STR: 0	BODY: 8
CHARGES: 75		
COST: 1435 HPs + $ 580M		

POWERS:
Telepathy*: 25, Warp: 25
* Telepathy has visual extension. Impulses can generate television images.

The Zone-a-Phone was a device which Superboy created from plans his father had left with the Projector when it was launched into space. It is essentially a large, TV monitor-like device connected to a large console.

The Zone-a-Phone allows someone in the real world to contact a Phantom Zone inmate. The Zoner can refuse to remain in the spot in the Phantom Zone corresponding to the monitor's location and thus prevent communications if he or she so desires. If a Phantom Zoner remains in the area to communicate, he/she appears on the screen as a ghostly white form against the background of the purple mists of the Zone. Any other inmate can approach the same spot and listen in and/or add their own comments.

With these limitations, it is not particularly effective and Superman rarely receives more than numerous

death threats from the Zone inmates when trying to communicate with someone. He uses the Zone-a-Phone to notify prisoners when they are ready to be released.

Much more sophisticated devices have been created in the 30th Century by such geniuses as Braniac 5, although the few remaining Zone inmates, by that time, are lifers and communication is even less necessary than it is in Superman's time.

SUPER-COMPUTER		
DEX: 0	STR: 0	BODY: 8
INT: 20	WILL: 10	MIND: 10
CHARGES: EPS		
COST: 1684 HPs + $ 124M		

SKILLS:
Detective: 5, Gadgetry/Identify Gadget: 10,
Medicine/Forensics: 16, Military Science/Camouflage,
Cartography: 12, Scholar: 12 (all fields of science, all eras of history, all Linguistic groups), Scientist: 16, Spy/Coding, Photo Interpretation: 5

The Super-Computer is an intricate device of Superman's own design. It is one of the most sophisticated computers on Earth and, if Superman were to patent it, he would probably make millions.

Superman uses his computer in the same way that most people would use theirs: for the accumulation and processing of large amounts of data, allowing him to use his super-intellect for other purposes.

The current computer incorporates Superman's researches into artificial intelligence. While it can reason and conduct its own investigations, it is nowhere near as "human" as the current Superman robot models. Its capability to make logical deductions and inferences based on stored data is almost unlimited and can seem truly miraculous to the casual viewer.

There is only one Super-Computer, located in Superman's Fortress of Solitude. Superman can access it from a remote terminal in Clark Kent's apartment, but his ability to enter new data and allow the computer to do a full analysis of objects is extremely limited in such cases.

AMNESIUM

Dex:	0	Str:	0	Body:	10
Charges:	34				
Cost:	1021 HPs + $ 1.9B				

POWERS:

Poison Touch (Special): 28

The exact origin of the substance known as Amnesium is not fully documented. It is apparently an artificial compound created by Superman, possibly from a Kryptonite isotope.

It is potent material, physically attacking anyone who comes within 10 feet (0 APs). The resulting APs of damage are not deducted from BODY, however, but represents APs of Information which the target loses from memory. It is the Gamemaster's discretion as to exactly which memories are lost but, in most cases, memories will be from the most recent on backwards in time. Approximately 23 APs represent one year of life experiences, but the GM may feel free to alter this figure at his discretion.

All current samples of Amnesium are kept by Superman in his Fortress of Solitude. He usually employs them to take away the memories of persons who have gained information of his secret ID or the Fortress of Solitude. Lead insulates against the effects of Amnesium and Superman has used bafflers of this material to reduce the APs of exposure, but it is still an inexact procedure. The Man of Steel is loath to use this material, and refrains from doing so unless no other option is available.

DISINTEGRATION PIT

Dex:	0	Str:	0	Body:	5
Int:	0	Will:	0	Mind:	0
Infl:	0	Aura:	0	Spirit:	0
Charges:	115				
Cost:	8472 HPs + $ 35.5Q				

POWERS:

Disintegration: 66

Created by Superman by the combination of a number of radioactive elements, this pit, approximately 3 APs deep, is used by the Man of Tomorrow to dispose of Kryptonite, various contaminated materials, etc.

The pit will attack anything dropped into it; damage to a Character is treated as Killing Combat (see the description of the Disintegration Power in *New Powers*).

FAR TO THE NORTH, IN THE UNINHABITED ARCTIC WASTES, STANDS A LOFTY CLIFF. IT LOOKS LIKE ANY OTHER ICE-ENCRUSTED ROCK MASS -- BUT HOW DIFFERENT IT *IS!* FOR A HIDDEN MIRAGE PROJECTOR CAUSES THE ILLUSION OF A SOLID ICE FACE, DISGUISING A LEDGE, WHERE A MASSIVE DOOR IS SET INTO THE SOLID ROCK. AND BEHIND THAT DOOR-- WHICH CAN ONLY BE OPENED BY A KEY SO HUGE ONLY *SUPERMAN* OR *SUPERGIRL* COULD LIFT IT FROM WHERE IT STANDS ON THE LEDGE-- IS THE SECRET SANCTUARY OF THE *MAN OF STEEL!*

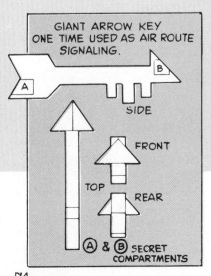

GIANT ARROW KEY ONE TIME USED AS AIR ROUTE SIGNALING.

A
B

SIDE

FRONT

TOP

REAR

Ⓐ & Ⓑ SECRET COMPARTMENTS

① SUPERMAN'S TROPHY ROOM

1st LEVEL

the FORTRESS OF SOLITUDE

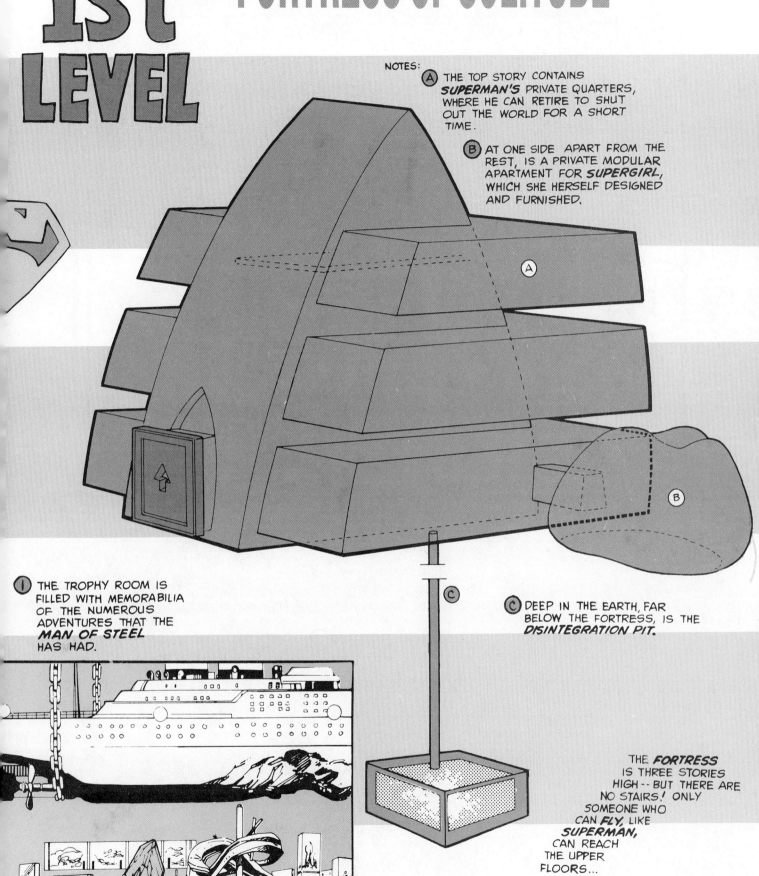

NOTES:

(A) THE TOP STORY CONTAINS *SUPERMAN'S* PRIVATE QUARTERS, WHERE HE CAN RETIRE TO SHUT OUT THE WORLD FOR A SHORT TIME.

(B) AT ONE SIDE APART FROM THE REST, IS A PRIVATE MODULAR APARTMENT FOR *SUPERGIRL*, WHICH SHE HERSELF DESIGNED AND FURNISHED.

(1) THE TROPHY ROOM IS FILLED WITH MEMORABILIA OF THE NUMEROUS ADVENTURES THAT THE *MAN OF STEEL* HAS HAD.

(C) DEEP IN THE EARTH, FAR BELOW THE FORTRESS, IS THE *DISINTEGRATION PIT.*

THE *FORTRESS* IS THREE STORIES HIGH -- BUT THERE ARE NO STAIRS! ONLY SOMEONE WHO CAN *FLY*, LIKE *SUPERMAN,* CAN REACH THE UPPER FLOORS...

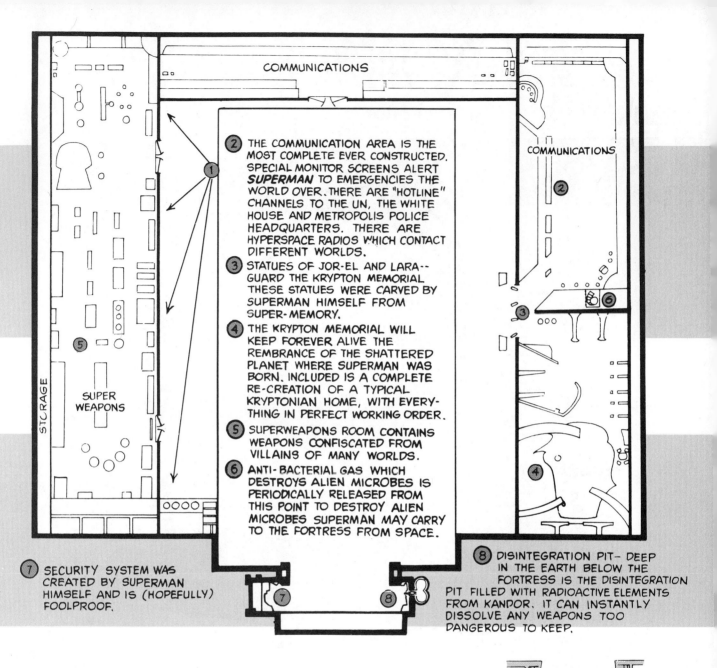

COMMUNICATIONS

COMMUNICATIONS

STORAGE

SUPER WEAPONS

(2) THE COMMUNICATION AREA IS THE MOST COMPLETE EVER CONSTRUCTED. SPECIAL MONITOR SCREENS ALERT **SUPERMAN** TO EMERGENCIES THE WORLD OVER. THERE ARE "HOTLINE" CHANNELS TO THE UN, THE WHITE HOUSE AND METROPOLIS POLICE HEADQUARTERS. THERE ARE HYPERSPACE RADIOS WHICH CONTACT DIFFERENT WORLDS.

(3) STATUES OF JOR-EL AND LARA-- GUARD THE KRYPTON MEMORIAL THESE STATUES WERE CARVED BY SUPERMAN HIMSELF FROM SUPER-MEMORY.

(4) THE KRYPTON MEMORIAL WILL KEEP FOREVER ALIVE THE REMBRANCE OF THE SHATTERED PLANET WHERE SUPERMAN WAS BORN. INCLUDED IS A COMPLETE RE-CREATION OF A TYPICAL KRYPTONIAN HOME, WITH EVERY-THING IN PERFECT WORKING ORDER.

(5) SUPERWEAPONS ROOM CONTAINS WEAPONS CONFISCATED FROM VILLAINS OF MANY WORLDS.

(6) ANTI-BACTERIAL GAS WHICH DESTROYS ALIEN MICROBES IS PERIODICALLY RELEASED FROM THIS POINT TO DESTROY ALIEN MICROBES SUPERMAN MAY CARRY TO THE FORTRESS FROM SPACE.

(7) SECURITY SYSTEM WAS CREATED BY SUPERMAN HIMSELF AND IS (HOPEFULLY) FOOLPROOF.

(8) DISINTEGRATION PIT– DEEP IN THE EARTH BELOW THE FORTRESS IS THE DISINTEGRATION PIT FILLED WITH RADIOACTIVE ELEMENTS FROM KANDOR. IT CAN INSTANTLY DISSOLVE ANY WEAPONS TOO DANGEROUS TO KEEP.

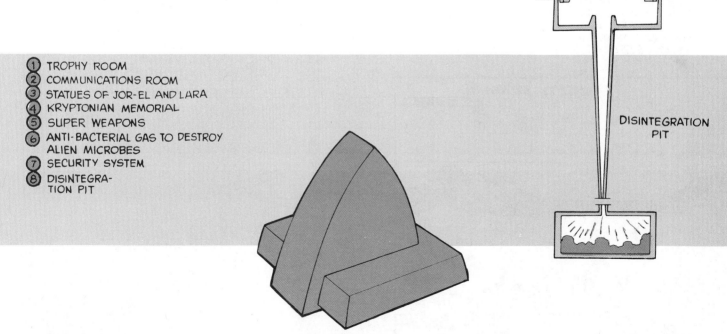

(1) TROPHY ROOM
(2) COMMUNICATIONS ROOM
(3) STATUES OF JOR-EL AND LARA
(4) KRYPTONIAN MEMORIAL
(5) SUPER WEAPONS
(6) ANTI-BACTERIAL GAS TO DESTROY ALIEN MICROBES
(7) SECURITY SYSTEM
(8) DISINTEGRA-TION PIT

DISINTEGRATION PIT

2 COMMUNICATIONS ROOM

3 STATUES OF JOR-EL AND LARA

4 KRYPTONIAN MEMORIAL

5 SUPER WEAPONS

6 ANTI-BACTERIAL GAS TO DESTROY ALIEN MICROBES

7 SECURITY SYSTEMS

8 DISINTEGRATION PIT

2nd LEVEL OF

① ARCHIVES

SUPERMAN'S FORTRESS OF SOLITUDE

CONTAINING THE MOST INCREDIBLE MIRACLE IN THE WORLD

THE BOTTLE-CITY OF KANDOR

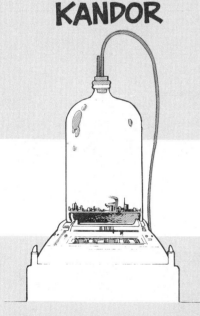

THE HORSE-SHOE-SHAPED SECOND LEVEL OF *SUPERMAN'S FORTRESS* IS A SCIENTIST'S DREAM.

THE ① ARCHIVES COMPUTER IS DESIGNED TO MAKE EVERY PIECE OF KNOWN INFORMATION AVAILABLE TO *SUPERMAN* AT A TOUCH. *(COMPUTER-LINKED UP WITH SUPER-COMPUTER)* TAPES ON ALL KNOWN PLANETS AS WELL AS ALIEN INFORMATION BANKS, WHICH CAN ONLY BE OPERATED BY *SUPERMAN*. SEATS 1 - TO SEVENTY FIVE.

② SUPER-COMPUTER - CAN STORE MORE INFORMATION AND DO MORE EXACTING WORK THAN ANY OTHER ON OUR WORLD. IT IS CONNECTED TO ARCHIVES WHICH INCLUI PERHAPS THE LARGEST CRIME FILES ON EARTH.

*

④ THE ALIEN ZOO HOUSES CREATURES FROM MANY DISTANT PLANETS AND CONTAINS ONLY THOSE ANIMALS WHICH THRIVE IN CAPTIVITY. THIS SMALL BUT UNIQUE ZOO HAS BEEN RESPONSIBLE FOR PREVENTING THE EXTINCTION OF AT LEAST SEVEN OF THE MORE DOCILE SPECIES OF ANIMALS ON OTHER PLANETS.

⑤ *SUPERMAN'S* LAB HAS SPECIAL EQUIPMENT MORE ADVANCED THAN ANYTHING ELSEWHERE ON EARTH. FEW SCIENTISTS COULD EVEN GUESS THE *USES* OF MANY ITEMS KEPT HERE.

⑥ THE *PHANTOM ZONE VIEWER* PERMITS *SUPERMAN* TO KEEP TABS ON THE *KRYPTONIAN* VILLAINS WHO WERE PUNISHED BY BEING BANISHED TO THAT TWILIGHT DIMENSION. NEARBY IS THE *(OLD-FASHIONED LOOKING BUT NONE THE LESS EFFECTIVE) PROJECTOR* WHICH CAN SEND ANYONE INTO INTO THE ZONE OR *FREE* THAT PERSON.

*③ THE BOTTLE-CITY OF *KANDOR*, ONCE CAPITAL OF *KRYPTON*, WAS SHRUNK AND STOLEN BY *BRAINIAC* BEFORE THAT PLANFT'S DEATH. *SUPERMAN* RECOVERED THE BOTTLE IN WHICH *KANDOR* WAS KEPT, AND PLACED IT IN HIS *FORTRESS* FOR SAFE-KEEPING. TANKS KEEP IT SUPPLIED WITH AN ATMOSPHERE EXACTLY LIKE THAT OF *KRYPTON*. IT HAS ARTIFICIAL GRAVITY AND A MINIATURE RED SUN, TOO.

A. ARTIFICIAL RED SUN.
B. CITY OF KANDOR.
C. SOIL AND RAW ELEMENTS.
D. UNSTABLE COMPOUND WHICH ORIGINALLY DESTROYED KRYPTON.
E. UNKNOWN BUT UNIQUELY KRYPTONIAN COMPOUNDS.
F. PLANET'S CORE ELEMENTS.

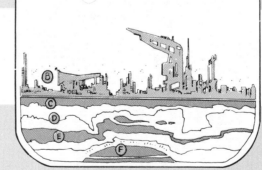

④ ZOO

⑤ SUPER-LAB

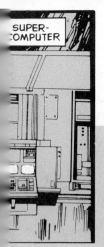

SUPER-
COMPUTER

③ THE BOTTLE-CITY OF KANDOR
EXTERIOR AND INTERIOR

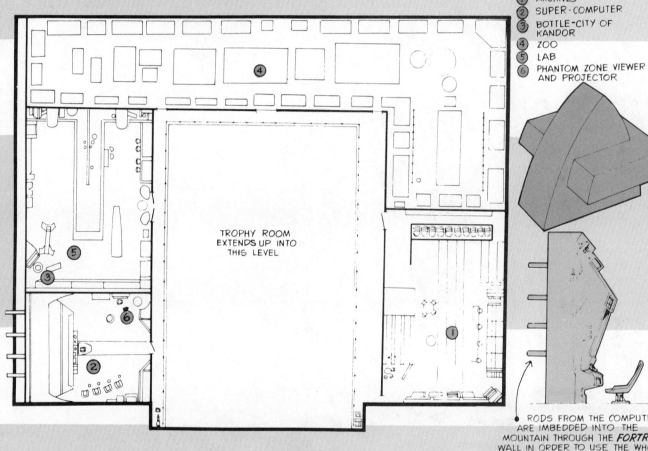

TROPHY ROOM
EXTENDS UP INTO
THIS LEVEL

① ARCHIVES
② SUPER-COMPUTER
③ BOTTLE-CITY OF
   KANDOR
④ ZOO
⑤ LAB
⑥ PHANTOM ZONE VIEWER
   AND PROJECTOR

● RODS FROM THE COMPUTER
ARE IMBEDDED INTO THE
MOUNTAIN THROUGH THE *FORTRESS*
WALL IN ORDER TO USE THE WHOLE
MOUNTAIN RANGE AS AN AERIAL FOR
THE COMPUTER AND THE DEVICES ON
THE THIRD LEVEL.

⑥ PHANTOM ZONE
VIEWER AND
PROJECTOR

EARTH-2

SUPERMAN

HEAR THAT, BABY? THAT'S YOUR NEW NAME... CLARK KENT!

WAYNE BORING & JERRY ORDWAY

The Earth-2 universe was the comic-book world of the 1940's and World War II. Heroes such as the Justice Society of America, the All-Star Squadron, and the Jay Garrick Flash existed here . The most widely acclaimed hero of Earth-2, though, was the original Superman.

The Earth-2 Superman was not as powerful as his Pre-Crisis counterpart. However, he has the same origins as his other incarnations; he, too, came from the planet Krypton.

On the Earth-2 Krypton, all of the natives possessed powers, although these were limited by Krypton's high gravity. One of the leading scientists, Jor-El, was unable to convince the ruling Science Council that the planet's destruction was imminent. However, Jor-El was able to send his son safely away in an experimental rocket just in time.

John and Mary Kent were witnesses to the rocket's landing on Earth. Removing the baby from the capsule

moments before the fuel exploded, they took him to a local orphanage. They returned later to adopt him. The orphanage, frantic because of the strange child who was spreading mayhem with his strength and invulnerability, let him go with little fuss.

Mary and John named the child Clark Kent, and raised him as their own. Unlike his Earth-1 counterpart, Clark had no career as Superboy, but kept his presence a secret, gradually discovering and testing his powers under Earth's lighter gravity. John

Superman fought many strange opponents, including the malevolent Alexei Luthor and the power-crazed Ultra-Humanite. He accepted membership in the All-Star Squadron, and his ability to leap tall buildings in a single bound eventually evolved into the full-fledged Power of Flight. It was during a run-in with a con-man in which he was weakened by a strange green stone that he obtained the first clue to his true history.

Travelling fast enough to break the time barrier, Superman traced the green stone through space to learn its origin. Unable to exist twice at the same time, he witnessed the destruction of Krypton as a wraithlike phantom. He also discovered that he was Kal-El, the son of Jor-El and Lora of Krypton, and that this was how he possessed his strange powers.

Shortly thereafter, Superman was the target of a memory-loss spell cast by the Wizard. Forgetting his heroic identity and powers, Clark continued his heroics by fighting crime as a newsman; he no longer pretended to be timid. Lois, attracted to this "new" Clark, eventually accepted his proposal of marriage. She went on to discover his forgotten hero identity and got the Wizard to reverse his spell, but the couple mutually decided to remain married.

When George Taylor, editor of the Star, retired, Clark took his place and went into semi-retirement as Superman. He occasionally participated in Justice Society cases, and he vouched for his cousin Kara when she first arrived on Earth.

During the *Crisis on Infinite Earths*, the Earth-2 Superman's history, and the entire existence of Earth-2, was wiped out when the course of time was changed to allow only one Krypton. However, the Earth-2 Superman still existed. The Supermen of Earth-1 and Earth-2 battled the Anti-Monitor. After the Anti-Monitor's defeat, the Earth-2 Superman was reunited with his wife, Lois, who was saved from nonexistence by young Alex Luthor. As the anti-matter universe began to fall apart, the Earth-2 Superman, Lois, and the Earth-Prime Superboy travelled with Alex Luthor to an other-dimensional world from which there is no return.

Kent urged his adopted son to use these powers for good purposes.

Upon reaching adulthood, Clark donned a colorful costume and called himself "Superman." For his first deed as Superman, he prevented a public lynching of an innocent man and went to work on finding the real criminal. The story he wrote as Clark Kent was the key to his obtaining a job as reporter on the Daily Star, where he soon met reporter Lois Lane. Lois developed a crush on his Superman personna, but she considered the timid Clark Kent a weak-willed milquetoast. Lois' attitude made Clark reluctant to admit his own romantic feelings to her.

Rocketed to Earth years earlier than his Earth-1 duplicate, the Earth-2 Superman was heavily involved in World War II activities, but a great deal of his time was spent on the homefront. He joined with other heroes in the adventure that eventually led to the formation of the Justice Society of America, but declined full membership.

POWERS:

Flight: 45, Heat Vision: 30, Invulnerability: 48, Microscopic Vision: 11, Sealed Systems: 20, Super Breath: 20, Superspeed: 25, Systemic Antidote: 15, Telescopic Vision: 15, Thermal Vision: 15, X-Ray Vision: 20

SKILLS:

Artist/Writer: 4, Charisma: 16, Detective: 5, Gadgetry: 8

LIMITATIONS:

X-Ray Vision can't penetrate lead

VULNERABILITIES:

(All of Superman's loss Vulnerabilities affect his Attributes, Powers, and Skills)

Rare Fatal and Loss:
Green Kryptonite: Range: 3

Magic Miscellaneous:
all Powers, Skills, and attributes against magic (Mystical Powers or objects) are at 4 APs.

Miscellaneous Loss:
Gravity attacks subtract their RAPs from all of Superman's abilities, but his Abilities cannot be reduced below 0 APs.

CONNECTIONS:

Metropolis Police (high-level)
Metropolis Prison (high-level)
Street (low-level)
United Nations (high-level)
White House (high-level)

MOTIVATION: Upholding the Good
WEALTH: Affluent
JOB: Daily Star Editor-in-Chief
RACE: Normal Humanoid

EQUIPMENT:

SUPER UNIFORM		
DEX: 0	STR: 0	BODY: 25
CHARGES: NA		
COST: 991 HPs + $ 350M		

POWERS:

Skin Armor: 10

PSYCHOLOGY

Although Superman was Earth-2's first and foremost hero, both his powers and sense of responsibility developed gradually. For the first few years of his career, he was not above using intimidation and scare tactics to exact confessions and terrorize criminals. On several occasions, he seemed to feel that justice was best served with a criminal's execution by Superman's own hands.

In his early days, Superman was highhanded and, more often than not, outside the law. In one instance, convinced that juvenile delinquency was caused by shoddy living conditions, he demolished several evacuated government-built low-rent buildings, much to the consternation of authorities. Some time later, he declared war on reckless drivers by smashing several lots of dilapidated used cars into scrap metal.

As Superman's powers increased, his sense of duty and respect for the law did likewise. He grew into his role as Earth-2's champion, with duties far beyond simply fighting common crimes. Charity work and assisting in times of national emergency were now important to him. However, his fights with a newly emerging breed of villains took up much more of his time as well.

The Earth-2 Superman dealt with his Clark Kent persona differently than his Earth-1 counterpart did. The Earth-2 Clark Kent gave the appearance of a snivelling coward. In fact, the Earth-2 Superman himself referred to Clark Kent as Lois' "weak-kneed boyfriend" and a "cowardly weakling." He did not find it necessary to feign clumsiness as Clark Kent.

Unlike his Earth-1 counterpart, the Earth-2 Superman has only allowed himself one love: his wife, Lois. She is one of the few non-powered people with whom he can share his life.

METHODS

Although the Earth-2 Superman is capable of using his subtle sensory powers, these did not fully evolve until relatively late in his career. As a result, he tends to rely more heavily on his strength and invulnerability to obtain results than does his counterpart on Earth-1. He should not be underestimated, however, as he has been active since World War II. He is not scientifically inclined, but he is rarely outsmarted.

ROLE-PLAYING

Superman is not the super-scientific genius that his counterpart is. He is also much more direct in his response to any given situation. Having seen the destruction and carnage of a World War and the ruthlessness of such villains as Alexei Luthor, his views on life are somewhat more philosophical. He knows that good does not always triumph but, on the rare occasions when he doesn't succeed, he does not take it as personally as his Earth-1 counterpart does.

The Earth-2 Superman is fiercely protective of his wife, and can become enraged at threats to her person.

FRIENDS

THE SUPERMAN FAMILY

LOIS (LANE) KENT

DEX:	2	STR:	2	BODY:	2
INT:	2	WILL:	2	MIND:	2
INFL:	2	AURA:	2	SPIRIT:	2
INITIATIVE:	6	HERO POINTS:			10

SKILLS:
  Artist/Writer: 2, Charisma: 2,
  Detective: 2

WEALTH: Affluent
JOB: Reporter
RACE: Human

BACKGROUND

Born in the small town of Pittsdale, Lois Lane was determined to become a reporter from an early age. After graduation, she moved to Metropolis and got a job with the Daily Star. She moved up the ranks to become the paper's star reporter. However, she lost one of the biggest scoops of all times, the first appearance of Superman, to neophyte Clark Kent.

Enraged by what she believed to be his sheer luck, and further irritated by the overwhelming cowardice of her rival, she treated Clark with scorn. Their competition for stories became fast and fierce. At the same time, Lois grew enamored with the super-strong mysteryman who took Metropolis by storm.

Eventually, her attitude towards Clark mellowed to the point where she could see past her scorn to notice his absence whenever Superman was present. She spent a considerable amount of time trying to prove the two were one and the same, only to have all her efforts foiled.

During a period when Clark was suffering from amnesia and had forgotten his Superman identity, he became a new man: a brave, crusading newsman who fought crime relentlessly. Impressed and attracted to this "new" Clark, Lois eventually convinced him to propose. On their honeymoon she discovered his identity as Superman and helped restore his memory. Clark was insistent on their remaining married, even after his memory of his Superman identity had been restored.

When Clark was made editor-in-chief of the Star, Lois continued as head reporter, sometimes with the assistance of her husband's heroic alterego.

During the Crisis, Lois was supposedly wiped out of existence when the Infinite Earths recombined. In reality, Alex Luthor had rescued her from nonexistence and reunited her with her husband. The couple, along with the Earth-Prime Superboy, travelled with Alex to a paradisical dimension from which there is no return.

PSYCHOLOGY

Lois' main goal in life, at least until recently, has been to be the best at everything she is interested in. Until Clark Kent came along, she was the best reporter in Metropolis, and his frequent victories over her in obtaining scoops were a constant source of frustration for her. She also decided that if she was going to get married, it was going to be the "best" man possible. Thus her romantic, somewhat predatory interest in Superman.

Lois' attitude mellowed somewhat with time, to the point that she was able to accept Clark as a friend. It was when he was stricken with amnesia that she saw him without his affectations and fell in love with him. Although she has mellowed even more as a married woman, she still shows the stubbornness and courage that made her a star reporter decades earlier.

ROLE-PLAYING

Lois' "nose for news" will unfailingly lead her into trouble, but these days it is rare that she gets in over her head. She is an excellent detective, with keen instincts and perceptions.

Lois is a doting wife, but she is still her own woman. She feels that Clark would be lost without her. If he is in danger, she will come to his rescue as fiercely as he would if she were in trouble.

SKILLS:

Charisma: 2, Detective: 1

WEALTH: Comfortable

JOB: City Editor

RACE: Human

Employed at the Daily Star, James worked himself up from cub reporter to his current position over two decades. He rarely leaves his desk these days except for "special" stories. His instinct for a scoop is undiminished by age.

POWER GIRL *alias Kara/Karen Starr*

Dex:	28	Str:	33	Body:	36
Int:	8	Will:	19	Mind:	9
Infl:	10	Aura:	12	Spirit:	7
Initiative:	46	Hero Points:	145		

POWERS:

Flight: 37, Heat Vision: 25, Invulnerability: 28, Microscopic Vision: 11, Sealed Systems: 7, Super Breath: 20, Superspeed: 17, Systemic Antidote: 7, Telescopic Vision: 15, Thermal Vision: 15, X-Ray Vision: 20

SKILLS:

Scholar/Academic Study (Computer Science): 8

LIMITATIONS:

X-Ray Vision can't penetrate lead

VULNERABILITIES:

(All loss Vulnerabilities affect Attributes, Powers, and Skills)

Rare Fatal and Loss:

Green Kryptonite: Range: 3

Magic Miscellaneous:

all Powers, Skills, and attributes against magic (Mystical Powers or objects) are reduced to 4.

Miscellaneous Loss:

Gravity attacks subtract their RAPs from all of Power Girl's Powers, Skills, and Attributes, but these cannot be reduced below zero.

CONNECTIONS:

Infinity, Inc. (high-level)
Pemberton Industries (high-level)
Ultimate Computer Corporation (high-level)

MOTIVATION: Responsibility of Power

WEALTH: Comfortable

JOB: Software Designer

RACE: Human

Originally the cousin of Kal-El of Krypton in the pre-Crisis universe, Kara has but recently discovered her new, non-Kryptonian origin on the reformed Earth.

BACKGROUND

In the pre-Crisis universe, Kara was the daughter of Zor-El and Allura, natives of the Earth-2 Krypton. Zor-El was the brother of Jor-El (Superman's father) and the only other person to believe the scientist's claim that Krypton was doomed. Racing against time to build an escape craft, Zor-El was only able to build a ship that was large enough to save his daughter.

Unfortunately, the "symbio-ship" that Zor-El designed took a far longer route to reach Earth than did her cousin Kal-El's ship. It kept her alive, at a greatly reduced metabolic rate, and generated a hallucinogenic dream world to keep her mentally stable.

When her ship finally arrived on Earth, she was met by her cousin Kal-El, known as Superman on his adopted world. Kal-El helped his cousin get used to Earth and introduced her to human society. Although Kal-El was in semi-retirement as a hero, he vouched for Kara as a new member of the Justice Society of America. During the time she was with the group, she became a close friend of Helena Wayne, the Huntress, who helped her in preserving her secret identity and developing a life as Karen Starr. She joined Infinity, Inc. briefly when the group first formed and later struck out on her own.

Power Girl was one of the many heroes who fought the Anti-Monitor during the Crisis, and travelled back to the dawn of time. When the dust settled, her cousin Kal-El vanished in the anti-matter universe and the Huntress, her best friend, was dead. Also, as a result of the Crisis, she no longer had a Kryptonian heritage.

Several months later, Power Girl discovered her new heritage. While investigating her symbio-ship, she learned that it was a magical crystal.

Apparently, the high sorcerer of Atlantis, Arion, had sent his granddaughter 100,000 years into the future to prevent her use by Garn, Arion's evil brother. The paradoxical nature of the recombination of the Infinite Earths have made her that granddaughter, even though her basic nature was unchanged due to her presence at the Dawn of Time.

METHOD

With her headstrong nature, Power Girl tends to deal with most threats with her fists. She is not much of a thinker, lacking her cousin's vast experience, but recent events have taught her the value of restraint.

ROLE-PLAYING

Power Girl comes across as fiercely independent, self-willed, and somewhat "liberated." Part of this is due to her need to prove herself as a separate individual from Superman. Once she was accepted for herself, she became less overbearing.

ALEXEI LUTHOR *Deceased*

Dex:	5	Str:	3	Body:	5
Int:	14	Will:	4	Mind:	12
Infl:	8	Aura:	4	Spirit:	4
Initiative:	27			Hero Points:	130

SKILLS:

Charisma: 6, Gadgetry: 20, Military Science/Cartography, Demolitions and ECM: 9, Scholar: 10 (Chemistry, Computer Science, Electronics, Mathematics, and Robotics), Scientist: 24, Spy/Brainwashing, Coding and Photo Interpretation: 8, Thief/Security Systems: 8, Vehicles: 9, Weaponry/Exotic Weapons, Firearms and Heavy Weapons: 12

MOTIVATION: Power Lust
WEALTH: Multimillionaire
JOB: Criminal Scientist
RACE: Human
EQUIPMENT:

POWERSTONE *

Dex:	0	Str:	0	Body:	17
Int:	0	Will:	0	Mind:	0
Charges:	EPS				
Cost:	8620 HPs + $360T				

Power Drain: 55
(* see *Background* below for availability)

OMNI-GADGET

Class A:	2
Class C:	14
Charges:	NA
Cost:	* HPs + $160K

On Earth-2, a world in which relatively few villains have appeared, Alexei Luthor is indisputably the most infamous opponent any hero has had to face. His genius and ruthlessness are without equal.

BACKGROUND

Nothing is known of Luthor's background prior to his first meeting with the Man of Steel in Europe. He ran afoul of Superman while fomenting trouble between the small nations of Galonia and Toran. Luthor came perilously close to achieving his goals, but Superman emerged triumphant. He was unable to prevent Luthor's escape and the two soon met again when Alexei attempted to blackmail a U.S. city with a stolen earthquake generator.

Luthor struck over and over in the next years, each time with some new scheme to accomplish the downfall and subjugation of world civilization. It is unlikely that Luthor would have come so close to success if not for Superman's relative inexperience with his powers, which were still evolving during the years of their numerous conflicts.

Alexei caused Superman his greatest problem when the villain shared a cell with a con man called Dan Rivers. Rivers had discovered that, while passing himself off as a fortuneteller, he was able to "hex" Superman with the aid of a green gem in his turban. Luthor investigated River's story and, after locating a meteor of the same substance, exposed Superman's weakness to the world. Ironically, Superman was able to track down the initial source of the green material, which he called "Kryptonite," and discover his true origin.

Also around this time, Luthor gained the Powerstone, an alien gem which allowed him to drain strength from the Man of Steel and use it himself. Superman eventually defeated Alexei yet again, but the stone was stolen and used by the Ultra-Humanite against the All-Star Squadron. Its current location is unknown.

More recently, Alexei gained knowledge of the parallel earths and allied with the Earth-1 Lex Luthor against the Supermen of both Earths. This team-up with the Earth-1 Lex Luthor was Alexei's last known criminal scheme. During the *Crisis on Infinite Earths*, Alexei was summoned to Brainiac's command ship, along with many other villains from the various worlds. Thinking himself superior to the Earth-1 Luthor, he challenged the latter's role as field commander of the villains. Brainiac responded to this by killing Alexei.

METHODS

As a criminal scientist, the pivotal role in any of Alexei's schemes is played by some advanced scientific device. Although he usually expects Superman's interference, he rarely seems able to devise an effective means of dealing with the Man of Tomorrow. His knack for underestimating Superman is usually his downfall.

ROLE-PLAYING

In many ways, Alexei Luthor is the typical mad scientist, seeking to gain world domination. He is shifty and untrustworthy, with no regard for human life; he will cheerfully sacrifice his henchmen to make an escape.

ULTRA HUMANITE * (as a crippled man)		
DEX: 1	STR: 1	BODY: 1
INT: 16	WILL: 10	MIND: 14
INFL: 9	AURA: 4	SPIRIT: 4
INITIATIVE: 26	HERO POINTS: 90	

SKILLS:
Charisma: 8, Gadgetry: 18, Medicine: 14, Scholar: 12 (Chemistry, Computer Science, Electronics, History, Mathematics, Physics), Scientist: 23

LIMITATIONS:
Miscellaneous: Ultra-Humanite receives a -4 column shift to his OV when building robots, but he cannot spend Hero Points on any related die rolls.

* Ultra-Humanite (as Dolores Winters)		
DEX: 3	STR: 2	BODY: 3
INT: 16	WILL: 10	MIND: 14
INFL: 9	AURA: 4	SPIRIT: 4
INITIATIVE: 28	HERO POINTS: 110	

SKILLS:
Charisma: 8, Gadgetry: 18, Medicine: 14, Scholar: 12 (Chemistry, Computer Science, Electronics, History, Mathematics, Physics), Scientist: 23

LIMITATIONS:
Miscellaneous: He receives a -4 column shift to his OV when building robots, but he cannot spend Hero Points on any related die rolls.

EQUIPMENT:

POWERSTONE		
DEX: 0	STR: 0	BODY: 17
CHARGES: 20		
COST: 8620 HPs + $ 360T		

Power Drain: 55

Ultra-Humanite * (as a giant flying ant)		
DEX: 7	STR: 8	BODY: 12
INT: 16	WILL: 10	MIND: 14
INFL: 9	AURA: 4	SPIRIT: 4
INITIATIVE: 32	HERO POINTS: 125	

POWERS:
Acid: 11, Flight: 6

SKILLS:
Charisma: 8, Gadgetry: 18, Medicine: 14, Scholar: 12 (Chemistry, Computer Science, Electronics, History, Mathematics, Physics), Scientist: 23

LIMITATIONS:
Miscellaneous: He receives a -4 column shift to his OV when building robots, but he cannot spend Hero Points on any related die rolls.

Ultra-Humanite * (as a mutated ape)		
DEX: 11	STR: 20	BODY: 18
INT: 16	WILL: 10	MIND: 14
INFL: 9	AURA: 4	SPIRIT: 4
INITIATIVE: 36	HERO POINTS: 150	

POWERS:
Mental Blast: 13, Telepathy: 1

SKILLS:
Acrobatics: 7, Animal Handling: 4, Charisma: 8, Gadgetry: 18, Martial Artist/Taking a Blow: 10, Medicine: 14, Scholar: 12

(Chemistry, Computer Science, Electronics, History, Mathematics, Physics), Scientist: 23

LIMITATIONS:
Miscellaneous: He receives a -4 column shift on his OV when building robots; but he cannot spend Hero Points on any related die rolls.

MOTIVATION: Power Lust
WEALTH: Multimillionaire
JOB: Criminal Scientist
RACE: Human (originally)

With his ability to plant his brain (through surgery) into the proper body, plus his vast mental resources, the Ultra-Humanite is one of Superman's most tenacious foes.

BACKGROUND

Other than the fact that Ultra-Humanite gained his vast mental capacities and crippled body through scientific experiments, nothing is known of the power-mad genius' background. As the head of a variety of criminal operations, he came into conflict with Superman on several occasions. It first appeared that he was killed by his own electri-gun while trying to eliminate Superman.

Ultra returned, however. His assistants transplanted his brain into the body of actress Dolores Winter as per Ultra's recorded instructions. Ultra attempted to force a scientist called Terry Curtis to build him an atomic-powered disintegrator, but his plans fell through once more. He returned, leading a subterranean race, to steal the Powerstone from Superman.

Ultra-Humanite created two powered lackeys, Deathbolt and Amazing-Man, and gave nuclear powers to Curtis, who became known as Cyclotron. Ultra forced the scientist to work with him by holding Curtis' daughter hostage, then attempted to extort millions from the U.S. Government. Curtis and Amazing-Man eventually teamed up with the All-Star Squadron to defeat Ultra, but it was Curtis who sacrificed his life to seemingly kill Ultra once and for all.

It is not known whether Ultra returned during the war, but his brain was eventually transplanted into the body of a giant ant. More recently, Ultra arranged for his brain to be transplanted into a specially mutated great white ape. It was while he was in this form that he reassembled the Secret Society of Super-Villains. Later, Ultra attempted to gain revenge on the Justice Society and their children, Infinity, Inc.

After his most recent return, Ultra was launched into the sun on board a space shuttle during the Crisis. At this time, nothing further is known of Ultra since the recombining of all the Earths into one.

METHODS

The Ultra-Humanite prides himself on his incredible genius. His twisted, evil intelligence has produced an endless number of incredible schemes and the devices to fulfill them. Oddly, he lacks the talent to build good-quality robots. As a result, he usually employs a large number of lackeys to do most of his dirty work.

Ultra soon found out when he confronted Superman that very few normal henchmen last long. Consequently, his later plans included the creation of the electricity-wielding Deathbolt and the molecularly malleable Amazing-Man.

In recent years, Ultra was content to be a manipulator of others, as witnessed by his recruit of men and various villains into the Secret Society. He has also used the ancient Waters of Ruthlessness to cause various members of the Justice Society to attack their own children in Infinity, Inc.

The Gamemaster should keep in mind that, more than any other villain, Ultra will always have an escape route. His ability to return time after time (possibly in a different body but always with a new scheme of conquest) is his trademark.

ROLE-PLAYING

The Ultra-Humanite is undoubtedly strong-willed. Despite almost forty years of brain-shifting from man to woman to giant ant to great ape, he has retained an amazing degree of mental coherence for an insane criminal genius. A lesser mind might have cracked under the strain.

Like many mad geniuses, gloating is Ultra's favorite pastime, even though it is the revelation of his plans that usually brings about his downfall.

Like many major villains, he is an untrustworthy ally at best. Any partnership in which he is involved is guaranteed not to last long.

THE PUZZLER					
DEX:	4	STR:	3	BODY:	4
INT:	8	WILL:	4	MIND:	4
INFL:	3	AURA:	2	SPIRIT:	3
INITIATIVE:	15			HERO POINTS:	85

SKILLS:
Gadgetry: 7, Scholar/Academic Study (Games and Puzzles): 9

LIMITATIONS:
Catastrophic Irrational Attraction: Puzzles and Games

MOTIVATION: Psychopathic
WEALTH: Comfortable
JOB: Gambler, Criminal
RACE: Human

A twisted genius at solving puzzles, the man known only as "The Puzzler" put his talent to work committing crime.

BACKGROUND

Like many Earth-2 villains, the Puzzler's background is, in itself, a puzzle. He first appeared as a kidnapper and extortionist, capturing Lois Lane and threatening her life. Superman beat the Puzzler at a game of checkers, the stakes of which were Lois' life. The Puzzler later returned with a kidnapping scheme which fell through.

The Puzzler entered a card-playing tournament once, only to be beaten at blackjack, bridge, casino, hearts, poker, and rummy. His pride damaged, he swore a twisted revenge. He attempted to kill each of the champions in a way symbolic of that champion's game, such as bludgeoning the poker player to death with a poker. He was foiled in all of his attempts except one, and was then pursued to his lair by Superman. Although his hideout was filled with deadly traps, none were effective enough to stop Superman, and the Puzzler was captured. It is not known whether he has had any further brushes with the Man of Tomorrow, nor is it known if he exists in the Post-Crisis universe.

METHODS

The Puzzler's crimes always revolve around games. For example, he once attempted to take a table tennis champ's life. His puzzles are the basis for bizarre clues, which he sends to the Man of Tomorrow. The more devious his puzzles are, the better.

When committing crimes that require henchmen, the Puzzler will certainly employ lackeys, but he takes great pleasure in saving any killing for himself.

ROLE-PLAYING

Although the Puzzler considers himself a genius at creating and solving puzzles, he has yet to defeat Superman. Any crime he plans will be sure to climax in his facing Superman in some kind of game. He seems to get his kicks by challenging Superman to games; the Puzzler can't win, but he keeps on trying.

THE WIZARD *alas William Asmodeus Zard*					
DEX:	5	STR:	2	BODY:	4
INT:	8	WILL:	4	MIND:	7
INFL:	11	AURA:	14	SPIRIT:	7
INITIATIVE:	24			HERO POINTS:	90

POWERS:
(except as Secret Society member)
Animal Transformation: 4, Flame Project: 4, Hypnotism: 9, Illusion: 15, Lightning: 4, Spirit Travel: 6, Teleportation: 5

SKILLS:
Artist/Actor: 3, Occultist/ID Object: 8

VULNERABILITIES:
Attack Vulnerability — His opponents get a -1 column shift to the OV/RV of Physical Attack made on him

MOTIVATION: Power Lust
WEALTH: Comfortable
JOB: Professional Criminal
RACE: Human
EQUIPMENT:*
(as Secret Society member only)

CLOAK OF INVISIBILITY					
DEX:	0	STR:	0	BODY:	6
CHARGES:	NA				
COST:	202 HPs + $ 90K				

POWERS:
Invisibility: 12

ENERGY PRISM

Dex:	0	Str:	0	Body:	13

Charges: 20

Cost: 509 HPs + $ 1.45M

POWERS:
Reflection: 16

POWER GLOVES

Dex:	0	Str:	0	Body:	5
Int:	0	Will:	0	Mind:	0
Infl:	0	Aura:	0	Spirit:	0

Charges: 15

Cost: 102 HPs + $26,000

Magic Blast: 8

* Items reflect costs of building as gadgets, not occultist objects.

An accomplished magician and hypnotist, the Wizard has been a regular foe of the Justice Society for many years. He has sought revenge on Superman specifically on at least one occasion, and may do so again.

BACKGROUND

A petty petty gunman, William Zard decided that he would need to find a new way to commit crimes. Travelling to Tibet, he studied the mystical arts at a monastery. Here he learned black magic. Zard eventually killed his tutor and returned to America.

Taking the name of "the Wizard," Zard opposed the Justice Society. He gathered together several other Earth-2 criminals and called the group the Injustice Society of the World. They were defeated in at least two battles with the JSA; Zard sought out revenge on the JSA's individual members, including the Black Canary and Superman. It was during this time that Superman became amnesiac and married Lois Lane.

The Wizard was one of the Justice Society's most persistent foes. He was a member of the Crime Champions who battled the JSA and JLA. He travelled to Earth-1 to become a charter member of the Secret Society of Super-Villains, only to find his powers waning due to the dimensional crossover. He obtained several mystical artifacts to replace the faded powers.

Recently, Zard formed Injustice, Unlimited to oppose Infinity Inc. He was apparently killed by the new

Hourman, but this may have been yet another of his hypnotic illusions; his death has not been confirmed.

METHODS

Without his special equipment (which he abandoned several years ago), the Wizard has no taste for battle. He prefers to use any number of cunning illusions to confuse and distract his opponents. He has had many years of criminal experience and usually runs circles around younger heroes such as Infinity, Inc.

ROLE-PLAYING

The Wizard is a coward and a bully: he is gloating and triumphant when he has the upper hand, but he will run as soon as the tables are turned. He has little regard for his allies despite his membership on several teams, and he will abscond with the loot as soon as his partners are distracted.

INDEX

The first index lists the major Characters that are featured in this book. The page number given is where the Character's statistics may be found.

The second index lists the gadgets which are described in this book and where their statistics are.

The third index is a general listing of all of the major Characters, places, gadgets, and other noteworthy items in this book. In the case of a major Character, the page numbers given in boldface in this index indicate where the statistics for that Character may be found.

BY CHARACTER

PRE-CRISIS

GADGETS

GENERAL INDEX

NATURALLY, IT'S NEVER QUITE *THE END!*

ACTION TABLE

Opposing Value Columns

Acting Value Rows	0	1 to 2	3 to 4	5 to 6	7 to 8	9 to 10	11 to 12	13 to 15	16 to 18	19 to 21	22 to 24	25 to 27	28 to 30	31 to 35	36 to 40	41 to 45	46 to 50	51 to 55	56 to 60	61 to 65	66 to 70	71 to 75	76 to 80	81 to 85	86 to 90	91 to 95	96 to 100	101 to 105	106 to 110	111 to 115	116 to 120	+5
1-2	6	C	13	15	18	21	24	28	32	36	40	45	50	55	60	65	70	75	80	85	90	95	100	105	110	115	120	125	130	135	140	
3-4	5	9	C	13	15	18	21	24	28	32	36	40	45	50	55	60	65	70	75	80	85	90	95	100	105	110	115	120	125	130	135	
5-6	4	7	9	C	13	15	18	21	24	28	32	36	40	45	50	55	60	65	70	75	80	85	90	95	100	105	110	115	120	125	130	
7-8	4	5	7	9	C	13	15	18	21	24	28	32	36	40	45	50	55	60	65	70	75	80	85	90	95	100	105	110	115	120	125	
9-10	3	4	5	7	9	C	13	15	18	21	24	28	32	36	40	45	50	55	60	65	70	75	80	85	90	95	100	105	110	115	120	
11-12	3	3	4	5	7	9	C	13	15	18	21	24	28	32	36	40	45	50	55	60	65	70	75	80	85	90	95	100	105	110	115	
13-15	3	3	3	4	5	7	9	C	13	15	18	21	24	28	32	36	40	45	50	55	60	65	70	75	80	85	90	95	100	105	110	
16-18	3	3	3	3	4	5	7	9	C	13	15	18	21	24	28	32	36	40	45	50	55	60	65	70	75	80	85	90	95	100	105	
19-21	3	3	3	3	3	4	5	7	9	C	13	15	18	21	24	28	32	36	40	45	50	55	60	65	70	75	80	85	90	95	100	
22-24	3	3	3	3	3	3	4	5	7	9	C	13	15	18	21	24	28	32	36	40	45	50	55	60	65	70	75	80	85	90	95	
25-27	3	3	3	3	3	3	3	4	5	7	9	C	13	15	18	21	24	28	32	36	40	45	50	55	60	65	70	75	80	85	90	
28-30	3	3	3	3	3	3	3	3	4	5	7	9	C	13	15	18	21	24	28	32	36	40	45	50	55	60	65	70	75	80	85	
31-35	3	3	3	3	3	3	3	3	3	4	5	7	9	C	13	15	18	21	24	28	32	36	40	45	50	55	60	65	70	75	80	
36-40	3	3	3	3	3	3	3	3	3	3	4	5	7	9	C	13	15	18	21	24	28	32	36	40	45	50	55	60	65	70	75	
41-45	3	3	3	3	3	3	3	3	3	3	3	4	5	7	9	C	13	15	18	21	24	28	32	36	40	45	50	55	60	65	70	
46-50	3	3	3	3	3	3	3	3	3	3	3	3	4	5	7	9	C	13	15	18	21	24	28	32	36	40	45	50	55	60	65	
51-55	3	3	3	3	3	3	3	3	3	3	3	3	3	4	5	7	9	C	13	15	18	21	24	28	32	36	40	45	50	55	60	
56-60	3	3	3	3	3	3	3	3	3	3	3	3	3	3	4	5	7	9	C	13	15	18	21	24	28	32	36	40	45	50	55	
61-65	3	3	3	3	3	3	3	3	3	3	3	3	3	3	3	4	5	7	9	C	13	15	18	21	24	28	32	36	40	45	50	
66-70	3	3	3	3	3	3	3	3	3	3	3	3	3	3	3	3	4	5	7	9	C	13	15	18	21	24	28	32	36	40	45	
71-75	3	3	3	3	3	3	3	3	3	3	3	3	3	3	3	3	3	4	5	7	9	C	13	15	18	21	24	28	32	36	40	
76-80	3	3	3	3	3	3	3	3	3	3	3	3	3	3	3	3	3	3	4	5	7	9	C	13	15	18	21	24	28	32	36	
81-85	3	3	3	3	3	3	3	3	3	3	3	3	3	3	3	3	3	3	3	4	5	7	9	C	13	15	18	21	24	28	32	
86-90	3	3	3	3	3	3	3	3	3	3	3	3	3	3	3	3	3	3	3	3	4	5	7	9	C	13	15	18	21	24	28	
91-95	3	3	3	3	3	3	3	3	3	3	3	3	3	3	3	3	3	3	3	3	3	4	5	7	9	C	13	15	18	21	24	
96-100	3	3	3	3	3	3	3	3	3	3	3	3	3	3	3	3	3	3	3	3	3	3	4	5	7	9	C	13	15	18	21	
101-105	3	3	3	3	3	3	3	3	3	3	3	3	3	3	3	3	3	3	3	3	3	3	3	4	5	7	9	C	13	15	18	
106-110	3	3	3	3	3	3	3	3	3	3	3	3	3	3	3	3	3	3	3	3	3	3	3	3	4	5	7	9	C	13	15	
111-115	3	3	3	3	3	3	3	3	3	3	3	3	3	3	3	3	3	3	3	3	3	3	3	3	3	4	5	7	9	C	13	
116-120	3	3	3	3	3	3	3	3	3	3	3	3	3	3	3	3	3	3	3	3	3	3	3	3	3	3	4	5	7	9	C	
+5																																C

+5: One Column Shift for each +5.

C: Cancel. Each +5 row cancels one +5 column.

RESULT TABLE

Resistance Value Columns

Effect Value Rows	x	0	1 to 2	3 to 4	5 to 6	7 to 8	9 to 10	11 to 12	13 to 15	16 to 18	19 to 21	22 to 24	25 to 27	28 to 30	31 to 35	36 to 40	41 to 45	46 to 50	51 to 55	56 to 60	61 to 65	66 to 70	71 to 75	76 to 80	81 to 85	86 to 90	91 to 95	96 to 100	101 to 105	106 to 110	111 to 115	116 to 120	+5
1-2	+1	A	1	N	N	N	N	N	N	N	N	N	N	N	N	N	N	N	N	N	N	N	N	N	N	N	N	N	N	N	N	N	*
3-4	+1	A	2	1	N	N	N	N	N	N	N	N	N	N	N	N	N	N	N	N	N	N	N	N	N	N	N	N	N	N	N	N	*
5-6	+1	A	3	2	1	N	N	N	N	N	N	N	N	N	N	N	N	N	N	N	N	N	N	N	N	N	N	N	N	N	N	N	*
7-8	+1	A	5	4	3	2	N	N	N	N	N	N	N	N	N	N	N	N	N	N	N	N	N	N	N	N	N	N	N	N	N	N	*
9-10	+1	A	8	6	4	3	2	N	N	N	N	N	N	N	N	N	N	N	N	N	N	N	N	N	N	N	N	N	N	N	N	N	*
11-12	+1	A	10	9	7	6	4	3	N	N	N	N	N	N	N	N	N	N	N	N	N	N	N	N	N	N	N	N	N	N	N	N	*
13-15	+1	A	12	11	9	8	7	5	3	N	N	N	N	N	N	N	N	N	N	N	N	N	N	N	N	N	N	N	N	N	N	N	*
16-18	+1	A	14	13	11	10	9	8	6	4	N	N	N	N	N	N	N	N	N	N	N	N	N	N	N	N	N	N	N	N	N	N	*
19-21	+1	A	18	17	16	14	12	10	8	6	4	N	N	N	N	N	N	N	N	N	N	N	N	N	N	N	N	N	N	N	N	N	*
22-24	+1	A	21	20	19	17	15	13	11	9	7	5	N	N	N	N	N	N	N	N	N	N	N	N	N	N	N	N	N	N	N	N	*
25-27	+1	A	24	23	22	20	18	16	14	12	10	8	6	N	N	N	N	N	N	N	N	N	N	N	N	N	N	N	N	N	N	N	*
28-30	+1	A	27	26	25	23	21	19	17	15	13	11	9	7	N	N	N	N	N	N	N	N	N	N	N	N	N	N	N	N	N	N	*
31-35	+1	A	30	29	28	26	24	22	20	18	16	14	12	10	8	N	N	N	N	N	N	N	N	N	N	N	N	N	N	N	N	N	*
36-40	+1	A	35	34	33	31	29	27	25	23	21	19	17	14	12	9	N	N	N	N	N	N	N	N	N	N	N	N	N	N	N	N	*
41-45	+1	A	40	38	36	34	32	30	28	26	24	22	20	18	16	13	10	N	N	N	N	N	N	N	N	N	N	N	N	N	N	N	*
46-50	+1	A	45	43	41	40	38	36	34	31	28	26	24	22	20	17	14	11	N	N	N	N	N	N	N	N	N	N	N	N	N	N	*
51-55	+1	A	50	48	46	44	42	40	38	36	34	32	30	27	24	21	18	15	12	N	N	N	N	N	N	N	N	N	N	N	N	N	*
56-60	+1	A	55	53	51	49	47	45	43	41	39	36	33	30	27	24	21	18	15	13	N	N	N	N	N	N	N	N	N	N	N	N	*
61-65	+1	A	60	58	56	54	52	50	48	46	44	41	38	35	32	29	26	23	20	18	13	N	N	N	N	N	N	N	N	N	N	N	*
66-70	+1	A	65	63	61	59	57	55	53	51	49	46	43	40	37	34	31	28	25	23	18	14	N	N	N	N	N	N	N	N	N	N	*
71-75	+1	A	70	68	66	64	62	60	58	56	54	51	48	45	42	39	36	33	30	28	23	19	15	N	N	N	N	N	N	N	N	N	*
76-80	+1	A	75	73	71	69	67	65	63	61	59	56	53	50	47	44	41	38	35	33	28	24	20	16	N	N	N	N	N	N	N	N	*
81-85	+1	A	80	78	76	74	72	70	68	66	64	61	58	55	52	49	46	43	40	38	33	29	25	21	17	N	N	N	N	N	N	N	*
86-90	+1	A	85	83	81	79	77	75	73	71	69	66	63	60	57	54	51	48	45	43	38	34	30	26	22	18	N	N	N	N	N	N	*
91-95	+1	A	90	88	86	84	82	80	78	76	74	71	68	65	62	59	56	53	50	48	43	39	35	31	27	23	19	N	N	N	N	N	*
96-100	+1	A	95	93	91	89	87	85	83	81	79	76	73	70	67	64	61	58	55	53	48	44	40	36	32	28	24	20	N	N	N	N	*
101-105	+1	A	100	98	96	94	92	90	88	86	84	81	78	75	72	69	66	63	60	58	53	49	45	41	37	33	29	25	21	N	N	N	*
106-110	+1	A	105	103	101	99	97	95	93	91	89	86	83	80	77	74	71	68	65	63	58	54	50	46	42	38	34	30	26	22	N	N	*
111-115	+1	A	110	108	106	104	102	100	98	96	94	91	88	85	82	79	76	73	70	68	63	59	55	51	47	43	39	35	31	27	23	N	*
116-120	+1	A	115	113	111	109	107	105	103	101	99	96	93	90	87	84	81	78	75	73	68	64	60	56	52	48	44	40	36	32	28	24	*
+5		A	°	°	°	°	°	°	°	°	°	°	°	°	°	°	°	°	°	°	°	°	°	°	°	°	°	°	°	°	°	°	C

° For every 5 APs of Effect Value over 120, increase the Result APs by 5.

* Shift the Effect Value up one row for each +5 column and use the 120 Resistance Value. A 120 Effect Value against a 130 Resistance Value is resolved as a 110 against a 120.

A: All. The Result APs are equal to the Effect Value.

C: Cancel. Each +5 row cancels one +5 column. A 125 Effect Value against a 125 Resistance Value is resolved as a 120 against a 120.

N: No Effect. The action has no effect on the target.